Choral Music for Women's Voices: An Annotated Bibliography of Recommended Works

by

Charles C. Burnsworth

The Scarecrow Press, Inc.
Metuchen, N.J. 1968

Library of Congress Card No. 67-12064

Table of Contents

Chapter I
The Problem and Definition of Terms Used

A new surge of interest in choral singing in America has been well under way for the past several decades, spurred chiefly by the public schools and institutions of higher learning which have fostered choral singing experience. This interest has carried over into adult, nonacademic life. Following graduation, high school choristers and college choir singers have little difficulty in finding suitable musical opportunities in community and church choirs and glee clubs.

Even within this growth, however, there is prevalent a misconception to the effect that choral groups which are comprised of either all men's or all women's voices are necessarily inferior to choral organizations of mixed voices, at least in terms of available literature, if not in their very nature.

Although the literature available to the mixed choir is more extensive, the literature for all-male or all-female groups is neither meager nor inferior. An excellent repertoire of literature is available to both men's and women's choruses. In the specific case of music for women's voices, a diligent search can uncover a great body of truly good music originally composed for high voices.

Once aware of the extent of appropriate and available literature, the conductor of a women's choir can easily achieve the same degree of enthusiasm and dedication in his group as does the conductor of the mixed choir.

I. The Problem

Statement of the problem. It was the purpose of this study (1) to give a brief account of the history of choral singing by women, (2) to establish and validate a set of criteria for selecting outstanding choral works which were originally composed for female, or high voices, (3) to annotate each work selected according to the general content of its musical elements and style, (4) to provide catalog-type information which included number of parts, range, publisher, grade of difficulty and type of accompaniment, and (5) to establish and implement a system of multiple cross indexes of those scores examined.

Importance of the study. There has been a significant growth within the last several decades in the number of choral organizations comprised of women's voices. With this growth, the musical leadership of such groups has necessarily involved a great number of men and women with only limited knowledge of the available literature. There has been a parallel increase in the number of compositions written for treble choirs by contemporary composers, as well as the publication of previously inacessible works by earlier composers. All of these factors underscore the urgent need for a well-defined, selected bibliographical list.

II. Definitions of Terms Used

Choral music. "Choral music" was interpreted to mean part music, composed in two, three, four or more voice parts, but not to include canons, rounds, and single melodic lines to which a descant, or countermelody has been added.

Women's voices. The term "women's voices" has been interpreted to mean the "high" or "treble" voice parts of mature girls or women, in contrast to the lower male voice parts commonly referred to as tenor, baritone and bass.

Women's choir. A "women's choir" was interpreted as being a choral organization of female voices, and is synonymous in this sense with the terms "women's chorus" and "women's glee club."

III. Methods Employed and Sources of Information

The information included in this study was secured by means of examining the musical score of each work listed and, when possible, by hearing the work in actual performance. Also consulted were articles appearing in professional journals, unpublished master's and doctoral theses, and books and essays dealing with the topics of choral music and esthetics. Finally, the catalogs of most major American publishing companies and the invaluable Smith College publication (compiled by Arthur W. Locke and Charles K. Fasset) entitled "Selected List of Choruses for Women's Voices" were carefully screened.

IV. Delimitations

The primary purpose of this study was to examine and annotate only those works for women's voices which were scored as such by the composer. An occasional exception has been made to include a few works originally conceived for a boys' treble choir when both tradition and merit justify inclusion, e.g., Britten's "A Ceremony of Carols." A number of compositions originally scored for other vocal combinations, but subsequently arranged successfully for women's voices, have been listed but not annotated. Care was taken to eliminate the large mass of transient popular music and all other music of doubtful value. It may be assumed that each work listed, including arrangements, has met successfully the desired standard sought in the criteria of judgment described in Chapter Three and is, therefore, recommended for its musical value.

Works which appear in collections, and are worthy of inclusion in this volume, are listed under the appropriate title of the collection.

To keep the selection within reasonable limits, only those works readily available through American publishers and distributors were considered. Finally, opera choruses and music composed for other types of dramatic presentations were not examined in this study.

V. Organization of the Remainder of the Study

The second chapter of this study consists of a brief history of choral singing by women. Chapter Three details the formulation and development of the criteria used to select the musical works included in this recommended list. Chapter Four is devoted to a descriptive annotation of the works selected. Nine items of information pertinent to each selection are included. Foremost in importance to the conductor is the descriptive annotation of each musical composition. In the format adopted for presenting this information, the annotation will be preceded or followed by these items: composer, title of work, publisher and catalog number, number of voice parts and any solo assignment(s), grade of difficulty, approximate length, type of accompaniment if used, and the range from lowest alto note to highest soprano note.

Chapter Five is a series of lists which can serve as a cross-indexing for quick reference by conductors to all the information included in Chapter Four. Chapter Six contains a summary and conclusions.

of women explicitly:

> Women, too, weaving and parting the tangled threads with the shuttle, often sing a certain melody, sometimes individually and to themselves, sometimes all together in concert.[18]

In another statement attributed to him, St. John Chrysostom instructed, "This I say, not only that you may yourselves sing praises, but also that you may teach your wives and children to do so...."[19]

Yet another fourth-century Bishop, Gregory of Nyssa, described some female singing which he heard while visiting his ill sister, Macrina. He referred to the singing of the nuns at the mourning rite: "Virgins' voices singing psalms mingled with the lamentations were filling the place...."[20] Women also played a part in the secular music of this same period, although records are not as plentiful as in the case of sacred music. In writing of the Roman Empire of the late third century, Lang stated:

> The practice of music was not limited to men. Its vogue among women is seen in the writings of Lucian, who lavishes praise on the singing and cithara playing both of women of the aristocracy and of courtesans.[21]

Further corroboration can be found in comments by Pliny, a famous historian, and by Lucian, an important religious teacher. The Roman historian Pliny said of his wife, Calpurnia: "She takes my verses, sets them to music, and sings them to the harp." Lucian of Samasota, second century, described the musical customs of his times. The musicians he mentions are almost exclusively women, both amateur and professional.[22]

For a lengthy period after the fifth century, not much seems to be known about the musical performance of laywomen. Presumably they participated primarily in secular matters, although it is not altogether certain to what extent they were active even in this realm.

The performance of sacred music by women probably declined considerably, even within the convents and nunneries of the Middle Ages, although it was by no means eliminated. One reason for its decline was mentioned by Elson, who stated that the Synod of Antioch in the year 379 abolished the custom of permitting men and women to sing together.[23]

II. The Middle Ages

The extent of female choral participation in the Middle Ages is difficult to document. Two major problems beset the investigator here: first, general records of the times are either incomplete or unobtainable, and second, those which are available contain many contradictions.

E. K. Chambers, in describing a sixth-century wedding scene during the time of Queen Guinevere, stated that "women sang.... The men shouted...."[24] Queen Guinevere is even reputed to have composed some of the songs. But Chamber's statement does not make it clear whether this scene was associated with the sacred part of the wedding ceremony or the secular celebration afterwards. On the basis of other discernible facts from this period it would seem that the female singing had no place in the sacred ceremony.

It has been fairly well documented that public performance of religious music by women and girls was not allowed during this period. Drinker wrote:

> The liturgical choirs of girls, who preceded the boy choirs, eventually became cloistered in their own monasteries and no longer served in the public churches. Choirs of laywomen and girls, as well as of professional musicians, were absolutely forbidden. Congregational singing by women was also forbidden, even when they were in church with their families.[25]

The practice of using boys for treble melody parts was common. In the _New Oxford History of Music_ Handschin stated:

> In the first Roman _Ordo_, a ceremonial designed for the papal service and probably written in the eighth century.... we read that in the Easter Day vespers an Alleluia is sung with three psalm verses, after which an Alleluia is sung again with _melodiae_ by the boys.[26]

It is probable that only in the nunneries or cloisters were women permitted to participate in religious music. Plainsong was sung by these convent women and "became an earnest expression of their own spiritual life."[27] Drinker described their vocal training in this manner:

> The singing of nuns was a serious religious matter, sanctioned chiefly for the purpose of enhancing the value of prayers to the Almighty. Provisions were made for the singers to be properly trained. Each convent had its own nun-teacher. She was called _cantrix_, _cantorissa_, _sangerin_, or _singmeisterin_ according to the language of her country.[28]

This last statement suggests that both the singing and the training of the nuns were apparently widespread.

Often monasteries established for the seclusion of ascetic monks also included quarters for nuns. How often, if ever, these men and women combined their vocal efforts in praise of God during this early period is difficult to determine. It is certain that both groups separately engaged in frequent and earnest musical efforts, especially within the Benedictine order, which included among other interests a dedication to artistic pursuits. "From the fifth century until about the thirteenth," according to Drinker, "monks and nuns of the Benedictine monasteries often spent from five to eight hours daily in the practice and performance of liturgical song."[29] Such dedication resulted in high artistic achievement, attested to by numerous references in the writings of their contemporaries throughout the centuries.

Music, of course, was not the only field of artistic endeavor for these nuns. During the tenth century a learned German nun, Roswitha, produced six plays in Latin prose.[30] Smoldon suggests, however, that there is some controversy over whether the plays were ever performed in her own nunnery. Since this was the approximate time of the birth of liturgical drama, which normally employed music, it would seem logical to conclude that Roswitha's plays were, in fact, liturgical dramas. Further, most evidence suggests that nuns were not permitted to perform in early liturgical drama, thus the reason for the controversy referred to by Smoldon. It is his belief that they did not even participate in the famous _Quem quaeritis_ trope which dealt with the gospel account of three women approaching Jesus' tomb. He wrote, "Surviving rubrics tell us that three clerics are required to robe and hood themselves as women...."[31] The denying of female participation in the liturgical dramas may have been a common practice, as indicated by Drinker:

> Over and over again, nuns were forbidden to act in the liturgical plays. Women could not even reproduce the scene in which the three Marys visited the holy sepulchre on Easter morning. In all Europe and England, the Easter drama has so far been found in only six monasteries for women, whereas in the monasteries for men the play was never suppressed.[32]

The performers of the Quem quaeritis trope (liturgical drama) may have been at first limited to priests and choir boys, but as the plays developed and became disassociated from the Mass it is quite possible that nuns were gradually included. This detaching of the trope from the Mass and its subsequent move to the end of Easter matins were significant developments. The liturgical drama then achieved "a generous amount of literary freedom and developed into an authentic Easter Play,"[33] according to Young. He continues: "The move to the end of the Matins signalized details of costume and gesture--genuine impersonation."[34] Young's use of the terms "authentic" and "genuine impersonation" implies the possible use of women--nuns. Meese also observed, "About the year 1141 the places of the boy choristers were taken by adult falsetto singers...."[35] Whether the term "adult falsetto singers" refers to women or to male falsetto singers is not clear. Quite probably, his reference was to a specific community or location of performance and did not imply the use of adult falsettos as a general practice. Undoubtedly, performance practices varied as much as did the texts used in the various versions of this and other liturgical dramas.

The issue of women performers in secular circles of this period is less open to question for lack of documentation. For example, it is known that around 1050 Queen Margaret of Scotland "was famous for the ballads she composed and sang with her ladies-in-waiting."[36] During the ninth century the jongleurs of France and their counterparts, the German gänkler, began to appear. According to Reese:

> These men--and women--were often poor vagabonds who sang songs that others wrote, did tricks with trained bears or such other collaborators, animal or human, as might be at hand, found themselves

> especially in demand to enliven less elegant wedding festivities, behaved scandalously, and were in general the despair of the clergy.[37]

During a slightly later period, women were included also among the aristocratic poet-musicians of France. Reese wrote:

> The troubadours and trouveres were not wanderers like the jongleurs, but especially in the earlier years, persons of rank--noblemen, princes, occasionally ladies of high position. They flourished for some 200 years, from the end of the eleventh century to the end of the thirteenth, the best part of the Age of Chivalry.[38]

Included among their compositions were dramatic love ballads which were apparently mimed, therefore necessitating the use of women. Ritter further documents Reese's statement:

> . . . a number of ladies of rank, wives, sisters or daughters of troubadours, generally became trouveresses, as they were called. Marie de France and Clara d'Anduse were among the most famous of these.[39]

As secular female singing became even more widespread, the church eventually had to relax some of its rigid rules on sacred lay participation. As Drinker related:

> About the thirteenth century, one compromise was the introduction of congregational singing into the Roman Catholic Church. Religious words and familiar tunes that had never been silenced out-of-doors became formalized into hymns sung at the high festivals of Christmas and Easter.[40]

Women no doubt engaged in this congregational singing, as they must have participated in the responsories of the worship service. Within a century, the church also relaxed its formal pronouncement against secular female choral participation. Drinker detailed this evolution:

> Up to 1400 the Church had persistently refused to countenance anything but the high, clear singing of the Gregorian chants by the nuns. The rich, natural voice of the mature woman was considered to be outside the pale of decency. . . . But by 1400 the natural woman was coming into her own. . . . The Church was forced to yield to the popular will and tacitly condone the performance of pagan music under Christian titles in the form of. . . hymns and carols. . . . Everywhere the people were singing new folk songs, popular

> ditties, Christian carols, and spirituals--many of them composed by women and girls.[41]

The medieval town was instrumental in encouraging the growth of a strong secular community capable of influencing the local parish. Harrison wrote:

> The medieval town [of the fourteenth century] was a community behind walls.... Music emerged spontaneously, with its own style and forms, as an adornment of this [middle class] life and as the handmaid of divine worship. The home, the inn, the market and the street became the main centers of singing....[42]

While these concessions were being made somewhat informally by the churches, the nunneries continued to develop and encourage female participation in the more formal manner peculiar to them. After describing a number of manuscripts of liturgical dramas, many of which contain parts for the Marys, Smoldon related that "from the nunnery of Origny-Saints-Benoite [came] the fourteenth century St. Quentin drama...."[43] The implication is not only that women sang and portrayed these roles, but that they may even have written the drama and the associated music. An even stronger statement was made by Reese:

> The Las Huelgas MS contains a two-part exercise in solfeggio, the text of which shows that the piece was intended for the nuns of the convent. Yet the customary clefs are used. From this fact it may be deduced that neither the choice of the clefs nor the apparent tessitura indicates that works in thirteenth (or fourteenth) century MSS were intended for the exclusive use of men's voices. The clefs were chosen with a view of placing all the notes on the staff, and it is wholly likely that motets, conducti, etc. were sometimes sung by women--whether as nuns in convents or as trained or amateur singers in secular life.[44]

In other words, the position of the clefs in these early works does not necessarily indicate the voice to which the part was assigned. It was common, whenever the normal voice range exceeded the five-line staff, to introduce another clef or to simply alter the position of the original clef.

Since the Benedictine order was in part dedicated to artistic pursuits, the activity of Benedictine nuns in female choral performance is significant. An interesting source of information describing their practices in the late thirteenth century is a little-known manuscript written at Barking Abbey, an ancient abbey founded about 677 and the second English monastery for nuns. Entitled The Ordinale and Customary of the Benedictine Nuns of Barking Abbey, the manuscript was presented to Sibille Felton, Abbess of Barking, in 1404.[45] In addition to detailed rubrics, the manuscript contains valuable information about choral performances at the Abbey and includes liturgical directions for the presumably all-women choir. The general scope covers antiphons, psalms, chapters, hymns, collects, invitatories and responds. Several notes provided by Dame Lamentia McLachlan, L. S. B., shed some light on the nuns' singing. She says the singing of antiphons in the cloister is analogous to carol-singing.[46] Next she points out that the Ymeras agios sung at Barking on four festival days (Christmas, the Circumcision, the Epiphany and the Transfiguration) "was probably one of the very earliest pieces of plainsong to be harmonized."[47] Finally, she remarks that the Service of the Resurrection or of the Sepulchre,[48] a liturgical drama used at Barking Abbey, was like the Quem quaeritis in that it employed three Marys.

Even more detailed information about the choral practices of Benedictine nuns during the Middle Ages can be found in Hilpisch's History of Benedictine Nuns published in 1958. Hilpisch's comment on the significance of the chantress is as follows:

> The chantress was important: generally only one who had been especially trained would be chosen. She was not only, as today, a director of the choir but since there was much room for development in the liturgical life, she was expected to compose hymns and set them to music. Thus she had to be both poet and musician at the same time.[49]

This small volume makes it clear that choir singing in the convents was highly regarded not only by the singers but by those who determined the general procedures of convent life. As Hilpisch wrote:

> The religious life consisted first and foremost in the performance of choir service, which was given particular solemnity through the procession in the cloister and other practices.[50]

By the sixteenth century nuns were devoting a great amount of time to singing. "The canonical hours," Hilpisch observed, "were sung completely every day and current popular devotions were added."[51]

Parallel to this development, secular activity continued to flourish. In addition to many written statements describing the role of women in both sacred and secular music, numerous art works of the period document the growing participation by women, not only in vocal activity, but in instrumental music as well. A late fourteenth-century woodcarving from the Bambury Cathedral, as an example, shows a man playing a harp while a woman plays on a lute. The subjects appear to be members of the aristocracy. Two other art works showing secular activity are (1) Basano's (1510-1592) "The Artist with His Family", which depicts a woman playing a keyboard instrument and a woman playing a lute, along with five men and two boys and (2) "Group of Feminine Musicians" by an unknown French artist (c. 1520), which includes a flutist, a lutist and a singer. In a sixteenth-century tapestry, two of the three singers depicted are women, and the harpist included in the group is also a woman.

III. The Sixteenth Century

If the word "renaissance" can be interpreted to mean "the liberation of music from the bondage of the Church"[52], then the later Middle Ages may perhaps be called the beginnings of a musical "renaissance". While, as Lang expressed it, "the monkish theology of the early Middle Ages belittled women and considered them the most pliable tool in the hands of Satan, [it] was left to the Renaissance to reinstate women to human society...."[53]

Although the Church gradually became more permissive, the impetus for restoring women to musical performance was provided primarily, as has been seen, by secular activities. Drinker related that young girls of court families were groomed from childhood to marry into other rich families, in order to gain power and wealth:

> One hears of girls who learned Greek, Latin, Hebrew, philosophy, theology and medicine;

> girls who read the works of Plato,... Greek mythology, bible history... learned to make tapestry and to play the harp. Above all, they learned to make verse and to sing and compose in the new contrapuntal style.[54]

While some of these young girls married into royal families, many of their equally trained and musically gifted sisters did not, and chose the convent as an alternative. These highly trained singers, added to those who were receiving good training in the convents, greatly improved the level of artistic performance. Though some nuns' groups had been granted a few liberties in singing performances, the addition of members who possessed more diversified talents and interests gradually brought about more freedom. In Cologne, in 1550, according to Drinker,

> an edict was given out by the bishop that the nuns might act the parts of the three Marys in the Easter plays. In Italy, many convents produced sacre rappresentazioni.[55]

Choral singing by nuns evidently achieved a reasonably good standard of quality. Kinkeldey, for example, stated that "sacred music for high voices was much used in convents, in some of which the nuns often reached a high level of performance."[56] Female singing in the monastery chapels in the sixteenth century was so good, according to Drinker, that it attracted worshipers to these chapels instead of the regular parishes:

> At the Chiesa dello Spirito Sancto in Rome, the nuns sang vespers on Easter Monday with such perfection that the critic Pietro della Vallo said he had never in his life heard such beautiful music.[57]

Instrumental playing had also achieved a level of high repute among the religious sisters. Lang's account relates:

> Musical organizations founded and conducted by women were numerous, especially in Italy, and the religious in almost every convent were devoted to the music. They sang and played various instruments so well that the Venetians, Bolognese, Neapolitan, and Milanese public flocked to the evening services to hear their magnificent choral singing. The religious were not only engaged in the study and performance of sacred music but were skilled in all varieties of secular music.[58]

Though earlier composers may possibly have given some attention to the convents, the growing reputation of musical excellence among nuns aroused the interest of leading sixteenth-century composers. As Drinker suggests:

> It was for singers such as these that Palestrina, Lasso, Vittoria, Monteverdi, Couperin, Lotti, and other famous church composers wrote motets to be performed at special services.[59]

David lists several specific works as possibly having been intended for such groups, for example:

> Eleven of the twenty-one compositions of Palestrina's _Mottetorum quatuor vocibus partim plena voce at partem paribus vocibus liber secundas (1581)_ were for high voices, probably intended either for choir boys or for nuns.[60]

Emphasis on musical performance was increasing not only in convents but also in other areas of devotional practice, including the regular church service. This was due at least in part to the secular spirit which had permeated sacred music. Masses were frequently based on secular _cantus firmi_ or parodied from chansons, and the use of instruments and complicated polyphony became widespread. Secularism, however, was soon to have its influence on religious matters challenged by a violent reprimand from high church authorities. It came as a result of the Council of Trent in the middle of the sixteenth century and affected the choral practices of the nuns as well as church policies in general. In 1590 the convent at Kühbach in the diocese of Augsburg received a series of statutes directed at removing certain improprieties which had crept into the convents. According to Hilpisch, the laws began:

> First the religious service to which according to the teaching of our Holy Father St. Benedict, nothing is to be preferred, is to be performed devoutly in choir and elsewhere, with propriety, with complete words, with long pauses, with distinct syllables, with uniform voice, not one high, another low, in singing, reading and chanting.[61]

Musical performance in general had become careless. Polyphony undoubtedly made it difficult to understand the words, which in turn encouraged bad pronunciation, and the general attitude of the singers was irreverent.

Despite this apparent reversal, singing by women had become accepted by the church. The newborn Protestant churches also provided for female participation, mainly through congregational singing. The Lutheran service in its early years encouraged congregational singing, and in 1559, during Queen Elizabeth's reign in England, congregational psalm-singing was officially permitted.[62] Drinker even put forth the suggestion that there may have been Protestant female choirs:

> In the Calvinist churches in Switzerland and France there may have been trained women's choirs. Goudimel, in 1565, set eight psalms for four high voices. In his preface to the collection he says that he composed the music for both home and church use.[63]

Toward the end of the century in England, a dramatic change was made in the arrangement of the regular vocal parts in congregational music, which indicates that it was a widespread and quite acceptable practice for women to sing in the congregation. According to Harman and Milner, "the Psalter of Alison, published in 1599... is important in that the tune is always placed in the soprano part instead of the customary tenor...."[64]

Despite this impressive record of female musical endeavor within the church, secular opportunities for women in music were more important, plentiful and diversified. The normal pattern during most of this century was for women to perform only with women. According to Lang:

> In the actual performance of music, women seem to have been restricted to their own circle. Eminent soloists no doubt took part in madrigal singing and other intimate performances, but the preferred medium for alto and soprano parts was the boy's voice....[65]

One exception to the general pattern was observed by Reese:

> In Part I of the Dialogo della musica (1544) Antonfrancesco Doni gives the music of several madrigals, sung by the interlocutors, who are four men. In Part II, seven men and one woman sing compositions in varying numbers of parts.[66]

This is one of the rare references to joint male and female participation.

Women at this time also reached independent stature as musicians and several gained high fame. Chief among them was Isabelle d'Este, whom Lang describes as "the most accomplished [female] figure, the perfect dilettante, the very _donna universale_ of the Renaissance ideal...."[67] Other women also came into prominence, as noted by Reese:

> In 1583 Giaches de Wert began his visits to Ferrara. Here he fell in love with Targuinia Molza, who, with Laura Peperara and Lucrezia Bendidio, took part in celebrated concerts of women performers at the court of the Este. Targuinia was composer, conductor, singer and instrumentalist in the court....[68]

In a significant account, Harman and Milner mentioned the same three women:

> The fame of these three [ladies] spread far beyond Ferrara and even beyond Italy, and Alfonso, [II, head of the Ferrarese court 1558-1597] fully aware of this and knowing that attempts had been made to find out what kind of music they sang and how they sang it, forbade the publication of their repertoire.... Among the numerous composers who paid homage to the three ladies was Claudio Monteverdi.[69]

Interest in instrumental playing by women, which began in the fourteenth and fifteenth centuries, was also growing. Reese stated:

> The thousands of pilgrims who came to Cologne annually from all along the Rhine early in the sixteenth century included musicians.... Among the several female singers named in contemporary records are some who also played instruments.[70]

At least three other prominent women musicians were listed by Drinker as "Lucrezia Tuornabuoni [who] composed Christmas carols... Margaret of Austria [who] made beautiful love songs [and] Anne Boleyn [who] could dance and sing [and] play the lute."[71] Among women composers of this period, listed by Elson were Maddalena Caulana, who published two volumes of madrigals in 1568 and 1583; Vittoria Alcotti, who published _Chirlanda dei Madrigali a 4_ voci in 1593; and Francesca Caccini (b. 1581), who was the daughter of the famed Florentine and who possessed a great singing and composing talent.[72]

Women composers of a slightly later era whom Elson included were Barbara Strozzi, who had an opera produced in Venice in 1695; Cattarina Assandra (c. 1600), who wrote a two voice Veni Sancte Spiritus; and Cornelia Calegari (b. 1644), who sang, played organ motets at the age of fifteen and wrote several masses for six voices and instruments.[73]

Among works specifically written for women, Hans David cites Louange et gloire by Henry Lecouteux as one of the few extant examples of early polyphony.[74] It was first performed in 1551 during a pageant at Rouen honoring King Henry II of France and Queen Catherine de 'Medici. In the festive procession, it was sung by "the worthy ladies sitting in the float of Religion."[75] The same composition was described by Drinker:

> When King Henry II of France travelled to Rouen, he too was entertained by a pageant. The chronicle of the festival describes a slow chariot on which ladies representing Vesta, Royal Dignity, Triumphant Virtue, Respect, and Awe rode while they sang a song of praise to the king. The very words and music that they sang are still in existence--a four part motet for three soprano voices and one alto by H. Lecouteux.[76]

This procession was also the subject of a painting by Cassoni, which further documents not only the event, but the female choir performance.

IV. Castrati Singers

During the sixteenth century and for a considerable period afterwards castrati singers gained increased prominence. There are conflicting statements regarding their origin. Bowman, for example, made the following observation:

> The origin of the castrato voice seems to be entirely obscure, as only a few facts can be found regarding it prior to its prevalence in Italian opera seria during the seventeenth and eighteenth centuries.... We have no trustworthy information on whether castrati were used in the earliest church music.[77]

The practice may be centuries old. Lang had reasons for thinking that "the origin of castration for the sake of a musical career goes back to age-old Oriental practices."[78] The rise in importance of castrati singers at this time must be attributed generally to the needs of both opera and the church. According to Bowman:

> There were many reasons why the castrato appeared on the scene and why he was able to reach such heights of glory and fame. Probably one of the most important sociological reasons was the exclusion of women from the choirs of the Roman Church. Boys' voices could be substituted for women's voices, as now, but there was one serious drawback--their voices were very short-lived.[79]

Although castration for musical purposes was a controversial moral issue, castrates were extensively employed in nearly all of Europe except France, where the practice was considered an affront against nature. Bowman wrote:

> Even in puritan England, the artificial male soprano held the center of the stage for nearly two centuries. The castrati were masters over their vocal organs and possessed power unattainable by women.[80]

Although the church had been neither the leader nor initiator in the development of female singing, but rather the follower of secular trends, this pattern may have been reversed in the use of castrates. Bukofzer stated that:

> The beginnings of the castrato practice were intimately connected with the Papal chapel in Rome where castrati appeared for the first time as early as 1562.[81]

Lang also gave the date of 1562 for the first entrance of castrati into the papal choir.[82] As might be expected, the influence of Rome quickly spread. Grout has written that "by the end of the seventeenth century, [castrati] were a usual feature in Italian churches in spite of periodic pronouncements by the Popes against the custom."[83]

Concerning papal condemnation of the practice of castration, there are conflicting statements. "By 1625," wrote Bowman, "the contraltini were superseded by the castrati and Pope Clement VIII declared officially that castrati for church choirs was 'Ad honorem

Dei' "[84] Lang, however, insisted that the practice of castration was never approved by the church, merely tolerated.[85]

By the late 1700's the incongruous nature of the practice was being condemned, for as Bowman related:

> The death penalty was provided for those who performed the operation and excommunication to everyone concerned in it--unless done (as often pretended) on account of some disorder and with the consent of the boy.[86]

Whatever the nature of the official position, castrati were employed in the Sistine Choir from the middle of the sixteenth century up to the nineteenth century, a long period of tacit church endorsement. The practice actually continued even longer, until Pope Leo XIII (1878-1903) formally ended the practice in Italy of castration for purposes of singing.[87]

The early writers of opera in the seventeenth century were quick to employ the castrati, but it must be pointed out that castrati were employed outside the church prior to the birth of the new art form. Biehl wrote:

> According to Michael Praetorius' report, the Munich Court (1560) had under Orlando di Lasso thirteen contraltos, fifteen tenors, and twelve basses, and along with them sixteen choirboys and five or six eunuchs. The latter make the small number of boys possible for each replaced two or three boys.[88]

Several sources list Monteverdi's Orfeo in 1607 as the first opera in which castrati appeared. An earlier opera, Euridice by Peri (1600), employed a natural soprano, Vittoria Archilei, and other accounts show that even in this newly rising field of musical endeavor, women were not altogether excluded. According to Bowman:

> There are not sufficient full records of the casts of early operas to enable us to trace fully the change from normal voice distribution when the musical drama began, to the abnormality of the casting of the male soprano in the leading role. The few existing examples from intermezzi and musical dramas of the sixteenth century show that the composers of that era treated the voices naturally.[89]

Even so, opera was soon dominated by the use of castrati.

In addition to Monteverdi, other leading composers who wrote for castrati singers included Cavalli, Cesti, Pergolesi, Scarlatti, Hasse, Handel, Gluck and Mozart.[90] There were many advantages to the castrato voice, some of which were detailed by Bowman:

> The singing apparatus of a castrato combined the larynx of a youth (emasculation prevents muscular change in this organ) with the chest and lungs of an adult. It therefore combined an unusually wide range with a sound of great power and of a special timbre which exercised great fascination upon the audience.[91]

Castrati could continue their careers for a long time; in some cases their quality, in Grout's words, "often remained unimpaired after as many as forty years of singing."[92]

The advent of castrati singing in opera resulted in a number of curious phenomena. Their popularity and their appeal caused the lower male voices to disappear almost entirely from early opera seria.[93] In addition to this, or perhaps as a result, castrates were assigned the feminine roles. That early opera audiences tolerated the seeming incongruity of male castrati taking female parts testifies to the fact that the audiences were mostly interested in vocal virtuosity, in which the castrati singers were supreme. The accurateness with which those roles were portrayed was not to be of major concern for some time.

The reign of the male soprano was in its glory in the days of Handel, and Italian opera still employed the artificial voice during the early years of Mozart's career. The role of "Siface" in Mozart's Mitridate as performed in Milan in 1770 was taken by a male soprano.[94] While castrati were used in the church well into the eighteenth century, in opera the practice soon waned. In Venice, as early as 1680, according to the French traveler Limojon de St. Didier, female singers were not only used, but were highly regarded. St. Didier wrote of the Venetian opera: "They commonly have the best Women Singers of all Italy...."[95] Harman and Milner mentioned at least three outstanding women opera singers during the so-called "golden age of castrati". Referred to as cantarices (i.e. virtuoso women singers), they were Francesca Guzzoni (1700-1770), Faustina Bordoni (1693-1781), the wife of Hasse, and Vittoria Tesi (1700-1775). Despite his predilection for using castrati, even Handel ceased to write for these singers after his oratorio Deborah.[96]

Gradually the art of the castrati declined, even in Italy. Perhaps this was due in part to a growing realization that the practice was monstrous. According to Lang,

> There was, however, another weighty reason for the return to a variety of voices ranging from bass to soprano and sung by persons of corresponding character, and that was the ever-increasing popularity of the opera buffa with its flesh-and-blood figures.[97]

As elements of realism came into Italian opera plots, male sopranos and contraltos were excluded. In Bowman's words:

> When dramatic verity claimed recognition on the stage the incongruous use of high voices had to be displaced by a normal distribution in which masculine and feminine qualities were appropriately displayed.[98]

The last important composer to write castrato roles was Rossini (1792-1868),[99] and with him ended a practice which lasted almost three hundred years. Women had once again survived an attempt to deprive them of responsible and natural participation in vocal performance.

V. The Baroque Era

Women continued their small role in public performance during the Baroque period in music. Despite the threat of the castrati, they not only became more active in music but gained increased public acceptance. In ballet, for instance, where at first only men performed, a woman ballerina appeared on the public stage as early as 1681 in Lully's Le Triumphe de L'Amour.[100] A woman appeared on the English public stage in a performance of Siege of Rhodes as early as 1656, an exceptionally early date for conservative England.[101]

The increased use of women in these and similar roles led to establishment of schools to train women performers. As described by Drinker:

> The demand for trained singers to take part in operas and oratorios prompted musicians to found special schools for the instruction of music. Hence, one of the new movements of the seventeenth and eighteenth centuries was the institution of schools for girls.... One of the first schools for the professional woman performer was founded in France

> by Lully.... In Hamburg, a municipal theater was established... and later, almost every city in Europe, England and the Americas had several conservatories of music which...expected the attendance of girls.... [102]

Out of the demand of such schools for suitable literature came a number of worthwhile compositions expressly scored for treble voices. Most notable among them are Dido and Aeneas by Purcell, written in 1689 for a boarding school for girls, and the Miserere of Hasse, written in 1728 for the girl's chorus at the Conservatio dege' Incurabili. According to Drinker, Hasse also wrote a "charming litany for the Empress Maria Theresa Vienna and her eight daughters to sing in their private chapel."[103] And Charpentier wrote his famous Christmas cantata for the young women at Port-Royal in the late seventeenth century.

These conservatories, many of them for orphan girls, were a milestone in the history of women in vocal music. Because of them a literature for women's voices arose, and much of the previous prejudice against women's choirs was overcome.

Performance of sacred music by nuns continued. The convents of St. Agnes and St. Christina had established quite a rivalry in the performance of liturgical song by the end of the seventeenth century, and according to Drinker, "the famous walk to Longchamps [Paris] originated in the eighteenth century as a pilgrimage of enthusiasts who went to hear the nuns sing the Tenebrae on Good Friday."[104]

To be sure, the Church opposed the appearance of women on the public stage and issued several decrees forbidding it. The decree of Pope Innocent XI, in 1676, was meant to prohibit this in the whole of Christendom, but it was not very successful either in secular or religious performances, as attested by the enthusiastic public response given to sacred music performed by the nuns. Paradoxically, as Ritter observed:

> ...though the church forbade women, throughout medieval times, and by actual prohibition in the sixteenth century, to take any active musical part in its services..., a feminine saint was adopted as patroness of music, and especially of church music... St. Cecilia. [105]

To the list of significant female singers in various ages must be added the names of Bach's second wife, Anna Magdalena Wülken, who was a Cöthen court singer, and Aloysia Weber, the sister of Mozart's wife. Both of these women established fair reputations as singers.

Few if any mixed choirs existed before the eighteenth century. Drinker, however, did list one such group as early as 1680--in France,[106] as might be expected, since that country never tolerated castrati. By the mid-eighteenth century, mixed choruses became somewhat more common, although as in the early hymn and psalm singing of this same general period, women usually sang only the soprano part. Said Drinker:

> In the first mixed choruses organized for singing oratorios, women sang only the soprano parts. Often, in public performances, they merely reinforced the choirboys' voices. In 1784 at the Handel commemoration in Westminster Abbey, for instance, eight ladies were permitted to assist the boys.
>
> . . . .
>
> The Stoughton Musical Society in America, organized in 1774, gave women the treble, but not the alto parts. Only gradually did the women take a natural place among the singers.[107]

It was not until nearly a century later that Mendelssohn and Spohr first assigned alto parts to women in a mixed chorus.[108]

VI. Complete Liberation

By the time that the Romantic movement was firmly established, after about 1840, small mixed choruses became common. Women were accepted members of such groups and the artificiality of male sopranos and contraltos in the performance of the new romantic songs and operas was no longer tolerated. By the middle of the nineteenth century, female participation in a fairly large number of secular choruses had successfully swayed public opinion concerning their acceptance into regular church choirs. Even in the Catholic church, women eventually were admitted to the religious choir--but not to a strictly liturgical choir--provided they sat in galleries at the back of the church. However, women were not, and are still not, admitted to membership in a wholly liturgical choir, be it Catholic or Protestant. Drinker distinguished between liturgical and non-liturgical choruses:

> ... Where church music is regarded as a kind of sacred concert... women are admitted to the choirs. But where music is a liturgy and the members of the liturgical choir are thought of as attendants of the priest at the altar, women are excluded.... This prohibition applies whereever there is liturgy in its ancient and traditional sense, in the church service--whether the church be Catholic, Greek Orthodox, Jewish or Protestant.[109]

Despite the general acceptance of women into mixed choruses, both secular and religious, the nineteenth century did not produce many outstanding women's choruses. Women's colleges gradually permitted amateur choral singing, and similar institutions associated with the church also served as centers where women and/or girls could function collectively as amateur singers. But suitable music was not much more readily available than it had been in the past. In fact, most of the choral literature written for women's voices in the nineteenth century is traceable in many instances to the directors of such choruses; it was often composed by those men who were trying to find music for their group to perform. Schubert, for example, composed some music for Nanette Fröhlick's pupils, and Brahms' famous Hamburg Frauenchör began from a simple request of one of his pupils to arrange some folk music for her and her two sisters to sing. The later significant contributions of Brahms to the repertoire for women's choirs were a direct result of his inability to find much suitable literature for the Frauenchör.

Women's choruses rarely performed on the public stage, even through the end of the nineteenth century. It must be remembered that the concerts given by Brahms and his young ladies were usually private affairs. Even in the United States, where women had gained numerous liberties, a public concert by a women's chorus in 1888 was not well received.[110]

The period following World War I saw a great acceleration in the development and public acceptance of women's choruses. This may have been partly due to the vastly increased number of girls' schools and colleges as well as the rise of women's clubs. But it must also be partly credited to Margaret Dessoff, who brought her women's chorus from Frankfort to the United States in 1912 to participate in a great German Brahms Festival, in which she won considerable public acclaim.

Largely due to the growth and improvement of collegiate groups, in recent years, the women's chorus is now recognized as a legitimate social and musical institution. As a result, there has been a considerable change for the better in both the quantity and quality of literature being composed for women's voices, especially by English, French and American composers.

---

1. Sophie Drinker Music and Women. New York, Coward-McCann, 1948. p. 63.
2. Ibid., p. 133.
3. Ibid., p. 71.
4. Albert A. Trever History of Ancient Civilization. New York, Harcourt, 1939. II: 595.
5. Drinker, loc. cit.
6. Ibid., p. 134.
7. Ibid., p. 137.
8. Ibid., p. 135.
9. Ibid., p. 160.
10. Ibid., p. 161.
11. Gustave Reese Music in the Middle Ages. New York, Norton, 1940. p. 63.
12. Drinker, op. cit., p. 160.
13. Reese, op. cit., p. 65.
14. Higini Angles "Gregorian Chant," New Oxford History of Music. New York, Oxford, 1954. II: 94.
15. Reese, op. cit., p. 68.
16. Jean Julian Dictionary of Hymnology. London, Murray, 1925. p. 206.
17. Arthur Elson Women's Work in Music. Boston, Page, 1903. p. 36.
18. Oliver Strunk (ed.) Source Readings in Music History. New York, Norton, 1950. p. 68.
19. Ibid.
20. Sophie Drinker Music and Women. New York, Coward-McCann, 1948. p. 68.
21. Paul H. Lang Music in Western Civilization. New York, W. W. Norton, 1941. p. 35.
22. Drinker, op. cit., p. 158.

23. Arthur Elson *Women's Work in Music*. Boston, L. C. Page, 1903. p. 37.

24. E. K. Chambers *The Mediaeval Stage*. Oxford, Clarendon Press, 1903. p. 235.

25. Drinker, *op. cit.*, p. 179.

26. Jacques Handschin "Trope, Sequence and Conductus," *New Oxford History of Music*. New York, Oxford University Press, 1954. II: 139.

27. Drinker, *op. cit.*, p. 190.

28. *Ibid.*, p. 191.

29. *Ibid.*, p. 190.

30. W. L. Smoldon "Liturgical Drama," *New Oxford History of Music*. New York, Oxford University Press, 1954. II: 219.

31. *Ibid.*, p. 179.

32. Drinker, *op. cit.*, p. 195.

33. Karl Young *The Drama of the Medieval Church*. New York, Oxford University Press, 1933. I: 13.

34. *Ibid.*, p. 223.

35. Arthur Meese *Choirs and Choral Music*. New York, Charles Scribner's Sons, 1911. p. 64.

36. Drinker, *op. cit.*, p. 208.

37. Gustave Reese *Music in the Middle Ages*. New York, Norton, 1940. p. 202.

38. *Ibid.*, p. 205.

39. Fanny R. Ritter *Woman as a Musician*. New York, Edward Schuberth, 1876. p. 7.

40. Drinker, *op. cit.*, p. 207.

41. *Ibid.*, p. 213.

42. Frank Harrison "English Polyphony," *New Oxford History of Music*. New York, Oxford University Press, 1954. III: 372.

43. W. L. Smoldon "Liturgical Drama," *New Oxford History of Music*. New York, Oxford University Press, 1954. II: 188.

44. Gustave Reese *Music in the Middle Ages*. New York, W. W. Norton, 1940. p. 323.

45. The modern edition is volume LXV of the Henry Bradshaw Society, published in 1927.

46. Caroling was an already established practice in the parish church and secular circles.

47. J. B. L. Tolhurst (ed.) *The Ordinale and Customary of the Benedictine Nuns of Barking Abbey*. London, Henry Bradshaw Society, 1927. LXV: 373.

48. Ibid., p. 378.

49. Stephanus Hilpisch History of Benedictine Nuns. Collegeville, Minnesota, St. John's Abbey Press, 1958. p. 35.

50. Ibid., p. 43.

51. Ibid., p. 55.

52. Willi Apel Harvard Dictionary of Music. Cambridge, Harvard University Press, 1960. p. 635.

53. Paul H. Lang Music in Western Civilization. New York, W. W. Norton, 1941. p. 301.

54. Sophie Drinker Music and Women. New York, Coward-McCann, 1948. p. 216.

55. Ibid., p. 223.

56. Otto Kinkeldey "Equal Voices in the Acapella Period," Essays on Music. Cambridge, Harvard College, 1957. p. 102.

57. Drinker, loc. cit.

58. Lang, op. cit., p. 302.

59. Drinker, op. cit., p. 224.

60. Hans David (ed.) The Art of Polyphonic Song. New York, G. Schirmer, 1940. p. 32.

61. Stephanus Hilpisch History of Benedictine Nuns. Collegeville, Minnesota, St. John's Abbey Press, 1958. p. 70.

62. Alec Harman and Anthony Milner Man and His Music. Fairlawn, N. J., Essential Books, 1959. II: 89.

63. Drinker, op. cit., p. 267.

64. Harman and Milner, op. cit., p. 91.

65. Paul H. Lang Music in Western Civilization. New York, W. W. Norton, 1941. p. 302.

66. Gustave Reese Music in the Renaissance. New York, W. W. Norton, 1940. p. 316.

67. Lang, op. cit., p. 301.

68. Reese, op. cit., p. 409.

69. Harman and Milner, op. cit., p. 3.

70. Reese, op. cit., p. 656.

71. Drinker, op. cit., p. 218.

72. Arthur Elson Women's Work in Music. Boston, L. C. Page, 1903. p. 65.

73. Ibid., p. 66.

74. Hans David (ed.) The Art of Polyphonic Song. New York, G. Schirmer, 1940. p. 34.

75. Ibid.

76. Drinker, *op. cit.*, p. 224.
77. Horace B. Bowman "The Castrati Singers and Their Music," (unpublished Ph. D. dissertation, The University of Indiana), Bloomington, 1951. p. 24.
78. Lang, *op. cit.*, p. 302.
79. Bowman, *op. cit.* p. 14.
80. *Ibid.*, p. 22
81. Manfred Bukofzer *Music in the Baroque Era.* New York, W. W. Norton, 1947, 1947. p. 399.
82. Lang, *loc. cit.*
83. Donald J. Grout *A Short History of Opera.* New York, Columbia University Press, 1947. p. 196.
84. Bowman, *op. cit.*, p. 29.
85. Lang, *op. cit.*, p. 354
86. Bowman, *op. cit.*, p. 75.
87. *Ibid*, p. 124.
88. Herbert Biehl *Die Stimmkunst.* Leipzig, Kistner and Siegel, 1931. p. 21.
89. Bowman, *op. cit.*, p. 31.
90. *Ibid.*, p. 91.
91. *Ibid.*, p. 82.
92. Grout, *op. cit.*, p. 196.
93. Bowman, *op. cit.*, p. 20.
94. *Ibid.*, p. 33.
95. Grout, *op. cit.*, p. 103.
96. Alec Harman and Anthony Milner *Man and His Music.* Fairlawn, N. J., Essential Books, 1959. p. 279.
97. Paul H. Lang *Music in Western Civilization.* New York, W. W. Norton, 1941. p. 449.
98. Bowman, *op. cit.*, p. 123.
99. Grout, *op. cit.*, p. 339.
100. Harman and Milner, *op. cit.*, II:171.
101. *Ibid.*, p. 184.
102. Sophie Drinker *Music and Women.* New York, Coward-McCann, 1948. p. 236.
103. *Ibid.*, p. 225.
104. *Ibid.*, p. 224.
105. Fanny R. Ritter *Woman as a Musician.* New York, Edward Schuberth, 1876. p. 8.
106. Drinker, *op. cit.*, p. 248.
107. *Ibid.*
108. *Ibid.*
109. *Ibid.*, p. 249.
110. *Ibid.*, p. 256.

Chapter III
Criteria Used for Selection

Selection of music for inclusion in this study is based on a number of criteria. Investigations in the related field of esthetics were the most helpful. Second in importance were the written opinions of recognized composers, performers and music critics. Third, the writer used his own observations of those elements which comprise a musical composition of high artistic merit. These observations, carefully analyzed, are based on a number of years of experience in conducting music scored for women's vocal combinations.

A fourth method for establishing valid criteria was that of submitting a preliminary list of criteria to a jury of recognized choral experts for their endorsement, amendment or suggestions as to validity. Such a method was used in a 1948 study by Christy but it revealed no significant differences between his own criteria and those arrived at by his jury of experts. Christy made two pertinent observations regarding his study. He concluded that "obtaining additional responses from similar judges could not be expected to change the results materially."[1] Secondly, he stated:

> It should be pointed out that the jury in this instance did not consist of a few random samplings from a much larger available group of similar character. It is considered improbable, if not impossible, to obtain another group of one hundred equally experienced and nationally recognized authorities in the United States. Since the possibility for further sampling of a similar nature appears to be well-nigh exhausted, it may be assumed that an adequate sampling of expert opinion was obtained and that the data thus secured approximate closely the data which would be obtained if the opinion of all possible judges of similar experience and standing were canvassed.[2]

For these reasons, the jury approach to forming criteria has not been used in the present study.

Selection of works for this list was made on the basis of what can be called an evaluative criticism, derived from an understanding of music esthetics, a term which applies more to the quality of a work than to its technical aspects. While some of the criteria employed are of a scientific or technical analytical nature, the criteria refer in general to the quality of the music and to its esthetic nature. While it may be highly desirable to establish a valid scientific measure of determining merit, worth or beauty, no such means has yet been devised. Scientific methods, such as the jury employed by Christy, can give a consensus on what works of art contain elements of merit and beauty, but cannot produce value judgments. Regarding this problem, Bernstein asked:

> Can anyone explain in mere prose the wonder of one note following or coinciding with another so that we feel that it is exactly how those notes had to be? Of course not. No matter what rationalists we may profess to be, we are stopped cold at the border of this mystic area.[3]

Studies in the field of esthetics or of evaluation of arts, such as those by Vernon, Burkhoff and others, generally set up more or less arbitrary examples of the expressive and the beautiful. However, Langer noted that:

> Works of art are not usually comparable. Only prize juries have to evaluate them with reference to some standard, which is inevitably arbitrary, and in many cases inapplicable. A competent jury does not even define a standard. If it consists of people who have developed their powers of perception with long conversance with the order of art (i. e. poetry, sculpture, music, etc.) in which their judgements are to be made, intuition will guide the verdict.[4]

Most studies dealing with attempts to measure appreciation in the arts emphasize the impossibility of obtaining an accurate standard for art evaluation. There is no general agreement on the meaning of such terms as "value", "merit", "good", nor even for the expression "work of art". Unsatisfactory as it may seem to some readers, it must be concluded that these are terms which, though undefinable, nevertheless carry with them a mutual empathic connotation among artists within a common discipline.

I. Intuitionalists and Rationalists

In analyzing a work of art, there exist at least two opposing schools of thought: the intuitionalists, who believe that beauty is self-evident and therefore cannot be analyzed, and the rationalists, who contend that things are beautiful because of formal structure which may be scientifically analyzed. Among those intuitionalists who maintain that the arts are incomprehensible by logic and therefore closed to scientific investigation is Max Schoen. Schoen defined the function of esthetics as follows:

> Aesthetics does not pretend to give a definition of an object of beauty, which would imply that any object that would comply with the specifications of the definition would be beautiful to any person coming in contact with it.[5]

Schoen's position may be described as the individualistic attitude to esthetics, for he maintained that the perception of beauty is a highly individual experience.

Rationalists, on the other hand, contend that since universality of approval or the "test of time" is what determines greatness, the value of a work of art is not individual, but social. Lalo seems to support this position; indeed, most writers who contend that art is created for an audience or that the essence of an art work depends unequivocally on shared experience with an audience would also uphold the social point of view.

The two opposing theories are described by Parker:

> Some thinkers have believed that there exist principles which can be applied to works of art to test their beauty with a certainty equal to that of the principles of logic in their application to inferences.... These principles, they would admit, are more difficult of application than the simpler logical rules, owing to the greater subtlety and complexity of art, yet, when found, have an equal validity within their own field. On the other hand, the view that there is no disputing about taste has never lacked adherents. According to this view, criticism can only be a report of personal, enthusiastic appreciation or repugnance without claim to universality.[6]

Both positions have much to recommend them, and in all probability both represent a degree of truth.

Yet, while most art works are conceived with an audience in mind, thus lending themselves to the social theory, art is capable of communicating to an audience only to the extent that the audience is responsive or is capable of being reached. Thus the work of art can be perceived only individually. Langer attested to this when she stated: "All knowledge goes back to experience; we cannot know anything that bears no relation to our experience."[7] In his "experiential" philosophy, Dewey gave emphatic support to this position. He said:

> To perceive, a beholder [or listener] must create his own experience... comparable to those the original producer underwent. The one who is too lazy, idle, or underrated in convention to perform this work will not see or hear. His 'appreciation' will be a mixture of scraps of learning with conformity to norms of conventional admiration and with a confused, even if genuine, emotional excitation.[8]

For many, the individual perception of a work of art will be the individual emotional experience derived from it and may be the only measure by which they may judge the art work. But such a position contains many inherent weaknesses, not the least of which is a lack of agreement on emotional meaning and significance. As Dewey argues, such a position leaves no provision for the education and cultivation of taste. Therefore emotional reaction is not a valid criterion for judging a work of art.[9]

II. Isolationism, Contextualism and Relativism

Fortunately, the issue of value standards has received considerable attention and a number of tenable theories have been put forth in recent years. Isolationism generally suggests the position of "art for art's sake" and may be thought of as the philosophical theory of the "discovered good". Schwadron suggests that in this theory the "structural insight remains the paramount criterion for standards of the ultimate good."[10] In other words, the significance of music is tonal, not extra-musical. It is not meaningful because it is descriptive or expressive of something. This position differs from the intuitionalist point of view in that the intuitionalists attach little importance to scientific or structural analysis. It is important to note, however, that the structural insight referred to in the isolationist point of view is acknowledged only in objective terms, not in subjective evaluations of structure.

Contextualism suggests the position of "art for man's sake" and may be thought of as the general philosophical level of the "received good". The philosophical theory of contextualism is generally based on a traditional reactionary level, essentially social realism. According to Schwadron, contextualism "stresses the spiritual context of music as expressive of life experiences"[11] and depends upon widespread social acceptance. The masses, not the experts, should judge artistic work. This position does not differ markedly from the rationalist point of view.

The third philosophical theory is that of relativism, which is a combination of the above two views. It recognizes the desire for improvement which can be brought about by education. It acknowledges the need for cultivating taste, yet admits to a plurality of tastes, and it confesses to the need for a system of critical standards, while permitting values to be culturally determined and of a relative nature.[12] Relativism permits esthetic criteria to be flexible and to undergo periodic re-evaluation. As Schwadron has indicated: a work of art should be evaluated according to the established or accepted criteria of the time in which it is being evaluated.

III. Points of Criteria

Faced with these differing viewpoints, the reader might justifiably ask, "Which theory has the most validity in judging musical worth?" Certainly, there can be no arbitrary disavowal of such influences as emotional appeal, experiential affinity and expressive content. These are all important considerations in evaluating a given selection, perhaps not in a scientific or syntactical analysis, but certainly in terms of obtaining the desired audience response to programing. Though it would be foolhardy to forbid their inclusion in establishing selective criteria, their role will be relegated to one of secondary importance in criteria to be established. Of first importance will be a leaning on isolationist theory, which emphasizes objective aspects of a musical selection, for herein lie more defensible and valid considerations.

Criteria established in the present study are as follows:

1. A high degree of merit as a work of art; that is, inherent esthetic beauty in a piece of music.
2. A text of literary value
3. Technical components well conceived.
   a. Elements of melody, harmony, rhythm and texture are interesting.
   b. Musical and textual phrases and sections are sensitively constructed and treated.
   c. Accompaniment, when employed, enhances the work.
   d. Demands on performers with regard to tessitura and acceptable vocal limitations (intervals and phrase lengths) are reasonable.
4. Probable appeal to both listener and performer.

A High Degree of Merit

There exist three areas of musical response and enjoyment: the sensuous, in which tonal combinations provide pleasures of sound; the associative, which induces thought connections to other ideas; and the syntactical, whereby the mind is stimulated by orderly tonal arrangements and relationships. All three of these areas are important, and most music involves all three, though usually giving emphasis to only one. But which is of more value? The position taken here is that the syntactical elements are the more important. Reimer supports this choice when he states:

> . . . while we might evaluate the response of listeners on the basis of weighing sensuous-associative and syntactical elements present in the response, we can only evaluate musical works syntactically. For the degree of presence or absence of sensuous and associative aspects in a piece of music is a completely subjective matter. Who is to say which piece has greater sensuous appeal or evokes the more poignant associations?[13]

Although subjective analysis or response must receive some consideration in determining this first criterion, the syntactical or objective aspect must receive primary importance.

Reimer outlines several interesting points pertaining to an

objective or syntactical analysis of a musical selection. He states that most persons recognize certain technical criteria for excellence in a musical work, such as consistency of style, clarity of basic intent, variety, and unity. But Reimer is quick to point out that these technical criteria may be found in many pieces of music which can hardly be labeled as "great", and that therefore their presence alone is not sufficient to differentiate real quality.

Essentially, a piece of music which has musical worth is one which possesses the important qualities of art: richness of imagination and invention, and intensity and lucidity of expression. Such intangible elements as expression, beauty, and human significance must also be considered. "A successful musical composition," writes Weinstock, "like every good work in any art... expresses pre-existing meanings and by so doing creates meanings that could not have existed before."[14] The work of art must communicate meaningfully, must "reach" or "get to" the listener in some manner. This perhaps explains why so many of the newer composition techniques, such as serial form, atonality, polytonality and others, are thus far relatively unaccepted other than from the standpoint of their intellectual aspects.

Within these newer forms and indeed, as far as their techniques are understood by the general public, there is little of a common bond of experience or emotional significance. Likewise, among many lesser composers and arrangers who continually flood the commercial market of choral music with "popular" and "novelty" selections, the presence of emotional elements in their efforts can hardly be discerned. On this topic, Thomson has said, "What makes possible the writing of good music, beyond that talent for handling sound that is required for being a musician at all, is emotional sincerity and intellectual honesty."[15] It would seem that the great composers of all ages have had both qualities in abundance.

The second part of Weinstock's statement, that a true work of art is capable of creating meanings that could never have existed before, is equally significant, and not unlike Langer's observation: "Just as words can describe events we have not witnessed, places and things we have not seen, so music can present emotions and moods we have not felt, passions we did not know before."[16] Lending credence to this comment is the remark of a friend, who in discussing his first hearing of the Bach Violin Concerto in E major, attempted to describe a rare musical experience. "After the slow movement," he said, "there was an incredibly long interval of absolute silence; of that dumbfounded silence in which men contemplate a revelation." Such is the power of a truly great work of art.

There are probably several valid ways to determine merit in a work of art. A number of writers have suggested that there are three facets of a work toward which a competent criticism of art must direct attention: first, the essential content of the work, its subject; second, the treatment of that subject, its form; and third, the human significance of the whole. Goethe shaped the same three questions thus:

1. What has the artist tried to do?
2. How has he done it?
3. Was it worth doing?[17]

Siegneur de Franeuse in the early eighteenth century considered this matter in a cleverly written dialogue between himself and an imaginary countess. In slightly condensed form his remarks are as follows:

> There are two great ways of knowing good and bad things; by our inward feeling and by the rules.... The authority of the rules is considerable, but after all it is not a law. Inward feeling is still less sure, because each should distrust his own.... I think that in this uncertainty and confusion the remedy is to lend to the inward feeling the support of the rules... and therefore I am persuaded that good taste is the most natural feeling, corrected or confirmed by the best rules.[18]

The rules to which he refers are rather simply stated:

> A piece of music should be natural, expressive, and harmonious.... These are the three great important rules which one must apply to the airs [music] that the inward feeling has approved.... A last rule, which must be added... is always to abhor excess.[19]

In the selection of music, at least two temptations often beset the conscientious choral director. First, he may be tempted to judge a piece of music solely on the basis of its composer, the assumption being that if the composer is one who is held in high regard, then the music must also be of high merit. As Quantz indicates, eighteenth-century musicians and critics were conscious of the dangers of such preconceived notions:

> ... we are usually inclined to begin by asking who the composer is in order to be guided by this in [forming] our judgment. Does the piece prove to be by someone to whom we have conceded our approval in advance, it is at once unhesitatingly pronounced beautiful. Does the contrary apply, or have we some objection to the author's person, the whole piece passes for worthless.[20]

That many works by composers of recognized (and revered) status are conspicuously absent from the recommended list in this study (see Chapter Four) should not be misunderstood as constituting merely careless omissions.

The second temptation is that of programing music because of its historical significance. On this point, Tovey states: "... the historical position of a work of art is not a matter of aesthetic importance. A work of art normally exists for its own sake and not for its position in history."[21] Various historical styles or periods may, of course, be represented on a program of choral music; but a piece of music must be regarded not purely from a historical point of view, but from an artistic one.

Of all the criteria one can use in selecting music, none is more important than this first one.

Any piece of choral music that commands serious attention from a conductor should be a work of art. Only when such a standard is clearly evident is the selection worthy of the time and energies of both performers and audience.

Text Which Has Literary Value

In judging music, the second and third criteria, literary value of the text and technical components, really cannot be considered apart from the general category of worth, for they are part and parcel of what constitutes worth. Even so, as important aspects of the total picture, they deserve at least passing attention.

There is danger that choral conductors may be misled into judging the merit of the text on the basis of its source. This situation is much akin to the temptation pointed out by Quantz of considering musical worth on the sole basis of the established eminence of the composer. Merely because a text by a man of recognized talent has been set to music is little reason to suppose that the end result is necessarily successful. It should also be kept in mind that the literature of choral music abounds with examples of hackneyed and completely unmusical settings of Bible verse, a text source of generally undisputed quality.

While the literary value of many texts may be spoiled by a poor musical treatment, much choral literature has enhanced a mediocre text by sensitive musical treatment. Langer has significantly observed:

> The measure of a good text, a good libretto, even a good subject for music, is simply its transformability into music; and that depends on the composer's imagination. Thus Mozart, working on The Seduction from the Serail, wrote to his father, who had found all sorts of fault with the libretto: "As for Stephanie's work, you are quite right, of course.... I know well enough that his versification is not of the best, but it falls in so well with my musical ideas... that I can't help liking it, and I am ready to bet that in the performance of the work you won't notice any shortcomings."[22]

Langer continues: "When a composer puts a poem to music, he annihilates the poem and makes a song."[23] That is why trivial or sentimental lyrics may be as good texts as great poems. Beethoven employed the greatest literature of his day, using Goethe, Schiller and their contemporaries, but Schubert often used decidedly second-rate material, such as that of Müller, in creating superb vocal music.

The degree of importance of text in choral music is one of curious dimensions. To the performers of the music, there is little quarrel about its significance, for they are involved with meanings, subleties, shadings and expressiveness and they are obviously aware of what the text says. Probably every choral conductor has experienced the frustration of working with a piece of music which fails to "strike the mark" in either rehearsal or performance. More often than not, the mystery is solved when he makes a careful scrutiny of the text and its rejection by the singers. But the importance of the text to the audience is not as real as the conductor might suppose. The truth of the matter is that, "when words enter into music they are no longer prose or poetry, they are elements of the music.[24] Auden also shares this view: "In song, poetry is expendable, syllables are not."[25] In The Pleasures of Music, Barzun reports on an experiment conducted by Vernon. Vernon discovered that a concert audience of average musical level took little notice of the text of a song performed. In a specific concert, sixty-three percent of the audience did not notice at all, and only six percent were definitely aware that the words sung to a song by Thomas Campion were nonsense.[26]

This is not to suggest that literary value of the text is of little consequence; it does illustrate that it is a factor of secondary importance in evaluating choral music. A good general rule when considering text as a criterion is Hirt's suggestion that the text should be "comprehensible and within the emotional experience of the singers, either actually or vicariously."[27]

The judge of choral music should look for an expressive treatment of both literary and musical elements, if he wishes to produce an entirely new creation which will be not only compatible, but uniquely artistic.

Technical Components

As in the case of the preceding criterion, the degree to which technical components may be regarded as separate factors in judging music is open to some question. Although effective handling of technical details is important, it probably has little significance in the ultimate value of the piece. The mishandling of such details, on the other hand, can hardly produce a work of art. About literature, Barzun writes:

> It has long been recognized... that true criticism does not consist in the exclusive analysis of an author's grammar and syntax. A poem is not judged or explained by listing the metaphors, constructions and idioms which it employs.[28]

Likewise, a painting is judged not solely on the hues of its colors, the lines of perspective, or the brush technique employed, but rather on the overall effect it creates. As Mendl stated the case:

> However closely we may analyze a work of art or discuss its technical characteristics, we can never bridge the gulf between technique, skill, science on the one hand, and spirit, emotion, imagination on the other.[29]

Similarly, an artistic piece of music consists of more than interesting chord progression, skillful counterpoint or complicated rhythmic patterns. It must have meaningful relationships and expressive content, sensitively presented.

Technical components are important to the general effect achieved, but the value judgment extends far beyond them. In this regard Tovey drew the following conclusion:

> ... the duty of the artist is not to contribute to an edifice entitled Art with a capital A. There is no such edifice. There are [only] individual works of art, and it is the business of each individual work to be a whole.[30]

If its import to a work of art is so minimal, why is this criterion even listed? Performers are constantly challenged to meet the technical demands placed upon them by composers but the only elements which the listener is even likely to be cognizant of are those of melody, harmony, rhythm and texture, and even these to only a superficial extent. What is more likely to be the focal point of most listeners is the sheer ocean of pleasurable sound in which he enjoys bathing. To the musically tutored, however, great art is more than a direct sensuous pleasure.

The technical components of a given work do then constitute an important part of a work of art, increasingly so when a higher level of understanding and beauty is sought. They may not always be evaluated or considered as separate entities, but the literature of music contains many examples wherein they may be so considered. The use of a Russian air by Beethoven in one of his Rasoumovsky quartets and Moussorgsky's use of the same air in his music-drama <u>Boris Godounoff</u> clearly emphasize that the element of melody in both works is a component to be evaluated. Likewise, the accompaniment of the Bach-Gounod Ave Maria must be evaluated as a separate component, especially when it is recognized that it exists as a separate work under the title "C major Prelude" in Bach's Well Tempered Clavier: Book I. The material used and the manner in which it is handled may directly influence or determine the actual life of a musical work, as well as its worth. Thompson wrote:

> Much music has been important to its own time because of its manner or details of its workmanship, only to fall by the wayside thereafter because the material was not of the quality to command admiration after the manner was no longer the vogue and when advances of technique had made commonplace the once admired workmanship. Other music has lived on because of the power and beauty of the material, when manner and workmanship came to be recognized as outdated.[31]

Technical components, like the text, must be judged by the conductor as integral parts of the work under consideration. While they may be evaluated individually for performance purposes, they must ultimately give way to esthetic evaluation of the whole. They are important, apart from their influence upon the performers, only as they comprise and complement the vitality of the art work. Thus they deserve careful attention in any systematic evaluation of a musical selection.

Probable Appeal to Both Listener and Performer

Initially it was thought that this fourth criterion, probable appeal to both listener and performer, should have no influence on the music to be included in this bibliography, for fear that the quality of the music selected might thereby be lowered. Happily, however, the general public has become far more sophisticated in its musical taste and has demonstrated its eagerness to hear good music well performed. More and more audiences seem interested in being esthetically nurtured rather than merely entertained. Thousands of amateur singers who once demanded popular music as a basic part of their repertoire are now performing music of more substantial quality. Conductors have discovered the truth of the recent axiom of composer Bacon: "In matters of public taste, no less than with the individual, it should be noted that just as liking something is conducive to doing it well, so also is doing it well conducive to liking it.'"[32] Indeed, among choral groups and their audiences an increase in the quality of the singing performance has often led to an increase in the quality of the music being sung.

Better quality music has greater appeal to both listeners and performers for the reason that great music is meaningful and significant to people. We may not be able to determine exactly what it signifies--an ambiguity which is actually one of the assets of music--but we know that it does convey meaning. Indeed, if it cannot express meaning, in all likelihood neither does it appeal to people, nor is it a work of art.

Certain composers have been accused from time to time of not keeping in touch with the general public and of writing for some cultural elite. Perhaps the obscurity of some composers may be traced directly to this cause, but it is hardly true of the great masters. Butler in writing of Bach remarks:

> It is imputed to him for righteousness that he goes over the heads of the general public and appeals mainly to musicians. But the greatest men do not go over the heads of the masses, they take them rather by the hand.[33]

Great composers are able to take the people by the hand precisely because they too as human beings have a knowledge of human feelings, and these feelings are what they are attempting to express. In writing of Monteverdi, Parry states:

> Monteverdi belonged to that strongly defined order of composers who are not so much impelled by the mere delight of music itself as by the opportunities it offers to interpret vividly emotions, moods, human feelings, dramatic situations, pathetic incidents and exhilarating joys. They are the musicians who instinctively feel music's sphere in the scheme of things. . . . they delve into human life and feeling, and get their highest inspirations from their keen sympathy with their fellow creatures and their insight into them.[34]

So it is, that these elements of expression are ever present in a work of art, and it is likely to be those musical works which contain such expressions which will have the greatest appeal to performer and listener.

---

1. Van A. Christy "Evaluation of Choral Music," *Contributions to Education.* New York, Bureau of Publications, Teachers College, Columbia University, 1948. p. 93.
2. *Ibid.*, p. 21.
3. Leonard Bernstein "Speaking of Music," *The Atlantic Monthly.* December, 1957. p. 104.
4. Susanne K. Langer *Feeling and Form.* New York, Charles Scribner's Sons, 1953. p. 406.
5. Max Schoen *Art and Beauty.* New York, MacMillan, 1932. p. 13.
6. Dewitt Parker *The Principles of Aesthetics.* New York, Silver Burdet Co., 1920. pp. 127-128.
7. Susanne K. Langer *Feeling and Form.* New York, Charles Scribner's Sons, 1953. p. 390.
8. John Dewey *Art as Experience.* New York, Minton, Balch, 1934. p. 54.
9. John Dewey "Meaning of Value," *Journal of Philosophy.* February, 1925. p. 131.
10. Abraham Schwadron "Interpretation of Philosophy and Aesthetics for Contemporary Music Education." (Unpublished Mus. A. D. dissertation, Boston University, 1962.) p. 176.
11. *Ibid.*, p. 77.
12. *Ibid.*, p. 93.
13. Bennett Reimer "Leonard Meyer's Theory of Value and Greatness in Music," *Journal of Research in Music Education.* Washington, Music Educators National Conference, Fall, 1962. X(2):92-93.
14. Herbert Weinstock *Music as an Art.* New York, Harcourt, Brace, 1953. p. 13.
15. Virgil Thomson *The Art of Judging Music.* New York, Alfred A. Knopf, 1948. p. 301.
16. Susanne K. Langer *Philosophy in a New Key.* Cambridge, Harvard University Press, 1951. p. 222.
17. Marlies K. Danziger and W. Stacy Johnson *An Introduction to Literary Criticism.* Boston, D. C. Heath, 1961. p. 251.
18. Oliver Strunk (ed.) *Source Readings in Music History.* New York, W. W. Norton, 1950. p. 491.
19. *Ibid.*, p. 493.
20. *Ibid.*, p. 579.
21. Donald F. Tovey *The Main Streams of Art and Other Essays.* New York, Oxford University Press, 1949. p. 161.

22. Susanne K. Langer *Feeling and Form.* New York, Charles Scribner's Sons, 1953. p. 160.
23. *Ibid.*, p. 153.
24. *Ibid.*, p. 150.
25. W. H. Auden "Notes on Music and Opera," *The Dyer's Hand and Other Essays.* New York, Random House, 1962. p. 473.
26. Jacques Barzun *The Pleasures of Music.* New York, Viking Press, 1951. p. 187.
27. Charles C. Hirt *Criteria for the Composing, Arranging and Editing of Choral Literature for the Senior High School Mixed Chorus.* Los Angeles, Affiliated Musicians, 1954. p. 7.
28. Barzun, *op. cit.*, p. 10.
29. R. W. S. Mendl *The Soul of Music.* London, Rockliff, 1950. p. 278.
30. Donald F. Tovey *The Main Streams of Art and Other Essays.* New York, Oxford University Press, 1949. p. 161.
31. Oscar Thompson *Practical Musical Criticism.* New York, M. Witmark and Sons, 1934. p. 57.
32. Ernst Bacon *Words on Music.* Syracuse, Syracuse University Press, 1960. p. 179.
33. Samuel Butler "Note Books," *An Anthology of Music Criticism.* compiled by Norman Demuth, London, Eyre and Spottiswoode, 1947. p. 99.
34. (Sir) Hubert Parry "The Significance of Monteverdi," *An Anthology of Music Criticism,* compiled by Norman Demuth, London, Eyre and Spottiswoode, 1947. p. 21.

Chapter IV
Recommended Compositions for Women's Voices

The musical selections for women's voices which appear on the following pages have been subjected to the critical standards listed and described in the preceding chapter and have been found worthy of inclusion in this selected list.

I. Works Included

There has been no attempt to make this list all-inclusive, although a large number of compositions were examined with great care. The vast bulk of arrangements of works originally composed for other vocal combinations were not considered to be appropriate to this study. However, a significant number of excellent choral works, particularly from the Renaissance period, and pre-existing melodies such as folk songs and carols have been successfully arranged for women's voices. Some of these have been listed, though not annotated, if they met the high standard of the established criteria.

The list also includes a number of compositions which were originally scored for equal voices, but not necessarily for women's voices. Often, according to the practice at the time of their composition, composers assigned many of these works to either high voice or low voice combinations.

Occasionally it was difficult to determine the original status of a composition whose modern edition indicates that it has been adapted, edited or transcribed for women's voices. In some cases this might signify merely a transposition of pitch or, at the opposite extreme, it might mean that an original SATB work has been edited to include the essential harmonies and vocal lines, but is now rescored for women's voices. Since little reliability could be guaranteed in determining the extent of those adaptations, only a small number of such compositions have been included.

In addition to the musical works included in this list, all of which are published separately, there are many excellent compositions which appear in collections. Those used are listed in the indices under the title of the collection.

Finally, there are many compositions originally scored for women's voices, which are intended almost exclusively for the Roman Catholic church service. Although many of these compositions are of acceptable musical quality, they have been omitted from this study because of their specialized nature.

II. Format of Annotations

The entry of each annotation follows the format described below:

Composer (arranged alphabetically by last name) — Publisher and catalog number of edition examined

Title of Composition

Number of vocal parts (solo assignments in parenthesis) — Grade of difficulty — Approximate length of composition

Descriptive Annotation

Type of accompaniment (if any) — Vocal range (lowest alto note to highest soprano note)

Other available editions (if any)

Arrangements which are included in this list specify the following information only:

Composer (or arranger) — Publisher and catalog number

Title of Composition

Number of vocal parts (and indication of accompaniment) — Name of Arranger or Editor

The abbreviations used for identifying arrangers and editors and the abbreviations used for identifying publishers, together with their addresses, are keyed and listed in the Appendix.

The durations listed for each composition should be regarded as approximations. Since ideas of tempo and interpretation vary, it was not considered practical to time each selection.

Publications containing several compositions, either by the same composer or different composers, will have each title listed in the same annotation. In such cases, the descriptive annotation has been generalized to include analysis of the publication as a whole rather than each work.

III. Explanation of Assigned Grades of Difficulty

The compositions listed have been categorized as easy, medium or difficult. These levels of difficulty were determined by a formula containing nine items of rehearsal or performance problems: (1) range, (2) melodic character of individual vocal lines, (3) harmonic elements, (4) rhythmic complexities, (5) complexities of text, (6) key signatures and inherent tonal relationships, (7) tempo, (8) physical demands and (9) accompaniment. Each of these items was considered in designating the selection as easy, medium or difficult in its musical nature.

What may prove to be difficult for one choir may well be easy for another, depending upon the abilities, proficiencies and capabilities of the choral organization. This grading system was applied on the hypothetical standard of what might be termed an average choir.

It is not suggested that this average choir would be found at either a high school or college level. Some high schools will have a choir that far exceeds this arbitrary standard, while many colleges may never achieve it.

The Average Choir

The following characteristics have been used to define what may be assumed to be an average choir:

1. A few sight readers who quickly grasp new music, comprising at least ten percent of the membership. They are essential to help the group hear the music in its early rehearsal stages and they serve to lead the others to a more rapid grasp and understanding of the notes.
2. A high percentage of members who learn notes quickly even though they remain somewhat dependent on the sight readers. They must be alert and rapid learners, so that the choir can sing confidently at an early stage of rehearsals.
3. Some familiarity and previous experience in singing literature of a nature similar to

that included in this study. Members are thus able to anticipate normal patterns of sequence, phrase construction and harmony and to transfer their knowledge to new works, permitting them to learn works with greater expedition and confidence.

4. Capabilities for hearing and listening to intervals, rhythmic patterns, harmony parts and accompaniment. Members who listen to their own chorus section, to the accompaniment, to interval leaps and to the other vocal parts relate their role to the music and significantly decrease the number of learning and refining attempts necessary.
5. Sufficient capability to handle reasonable ranges with ease. Sopranos and altos should have sufficient strength within their sections so that there is confident assurance that extreme fringes of their respective ranges will maintain both strength and quality.
6. Chorus sections which are strong and independent enough to cope with their own musical assignment while help is being given to other parts.
7. Sufficient confidence in the director, the various chorus sections and individual singers. Such confidence is important in minimizing hesitancy of entrances and in developing dynamic levels, blending efforts and chord tone members.
8. An accompanist who is technically capable and has a strong rhythmic sense. The accompanist should not attempt to be a solo performer, but must be a constant aid to the director and the singers in giving pitches, phrasing musically and presenting unfaltering rhythmic unity.
9. Patience, enthusiasm for the literature and a high *esprit de corps*.

No choir, of course, can rise above the technical capabilities and musical sensitivity of its conductor. The old adage that there are no bad choirs, only bad conductors is probably more true than is generally admitted. The standard of the average choir can be met or exceeded only to the extent of the conductor's musical endowments.

Graded Levels of Difficulty

The graded levels of difficulty of the music included in this study were interpreted as follows:

Easy

1. The range is undemanding, and highly contained in that it rarely exceeds a tenth.
2. The melodic movement of all voice parts is predominantly diatonic, with few leaps outside the chords, little if any chromaticism, and conventional melodic resolutions.
3. The harmony is confined largely to strong chords of a given key, such as tonic, dominant, subdominant and an occasional secondary dominant chord. If and when modulations occur, they are smooth and generally prepared by the accompaniment. Few if any chords contain any chromatic alteration, unless due to strong melodic type influences such as in contemporary music. Any counterpoint present is of the simple "counter-melody" type and is generally limited to two-part counterpoint.
4. Rhythm is fairly uncomplex and largely within the normal time meter accents. Few if any meter changes occur, unless a complete shift from duple to triple meter takes place. No compound meter signatures such as 5/4 and 7/8 are used. No syncopated rhythmic patterns or hemiola effects are used which would present rhythmic complexity. Dotted rhythms or similar patterns when utilized are not isolated changes in the established rhythmic flow, but used as basic patterns throughout much of the work.
5. The musical setting of the text is rather simple and metrically set to fit the basic pulse and the normal uncomplex subdivisions of the established meter. The text is understandable and within the "experience range" of the performers.
6. The normal diatonic pattern of regular tones and semi-tones of the established key is such that it presents no problem of recall.
7. Tempos are not too fast, permitting ease of note-reading and fitting of the text.
8. Little physical demand is made with regard to dynamic contrasts or phrase endurance.
9. The nature of the accompaniment tends to support the harmonies and rhythms of the vocal lines. When independent, the accompaniment still remains simple and complementary to the vocal lines.

Medium

1. The ranges employed often approach the normal limits which are considered safe for amateur singers. Usually, however, such notes are thoughtfully prepared by being well placed within the phrases and, in the case of high notes, well supported either by octave doublings or full chordal harmony by the lower voices. Passages which include notes in the higher and lower ranges do not dwell on these notes for any undue length of time.

2. Melodic movement of the vocal lines, including inner voices, remains predominantly diatonic, although leaps exceeding a third are common. Some chromaticism is normal, particularly within inner parts, as a result of more advanced harmonic progressions. There is more independence of parts, as a result of greater freedom from rigid homophonic writing.

3. Harmonic structure is more varied and non-diatonic progressions become common. Modulations are still relatively easy to manage, although enharmonic interchanges of notes are more apt to appear. Many of the harmonies employed still may be consonant, although some tendencies to linear writing result in more independence of resultant chord members. Not infrequently, dissonances occur, although they are usually resolved. Altered chords become more common.

4. Rhythmic freedom is increased and independence of part writing often results in varied and independent rhythmic treatment of the several vocal lines. Meter signatures are not so rigidly adhered to with regard to metrical accents, and such effects as simple hemiolas become normal. Meter changes may become more frequent, although they are normally the more common duple and triple types. Dotted rhythms, varied patterns and greater tendencies toward imitative writing often result in an unrigid approach to rhythmic matters, and the accompaniment often adds further independence to the rhythmic treatment.

5. There is more independence of vocal writing, especially in the use of imitative and contrapuntal techniques, which often results in textual complexities of a modest nature. Frequently, compositions of this grade level will have some polytextual sections.

6. Key signatures are usually not a limitation. Occasionally, some passages may temporarily modulate to other keys or new key signatures will be introduced as needed. Most of the part writing still remains related to the key signature of the moment, however.

7. Tempo limitations are not a consideration and occasional changes of tempo are rather common. It may be assumed that compositions with a more complex or independent treatment of text, and those compositions which involve more complex intervalic skips and relationships, are consciously tempered by the composer with a logical tempo which is in reason with any other complexities which may be present.

8. Dynamic contrasts or demands upon the singers may be more extended and general length of the work may be increased. Also, more refined vocal control may often be implied by works which contain more subtleties of nuance, phrase and shading.

9. Accompaniments very often may be considerably independent of the vocal lines and they may involve more precise and complex rhythmic alterations. It should be noted also that much more music of this grade level will be unaccompanied, thus increasing the responsibilities of the singers toward greater accuracy of rhythm, harmony and intonation.

Difficult

1. Range, with the possible exception of low alto notes, probably is of little concern to the composer. At least he does not consider it a limiting factor.

2. Melodic or linear movement of the individual vocal lines is generally freely treated. Chromaticism is often present. Difficult interval skips such as those of the diminished, augmented, sevenths, and minor sixths are quite common, particularly as a result of the modern contrapuntal style and advanced harmonic progressions which are often employed. Normal melodic resolutions may often be entirely ignored, resulting in angular lines. Frequent parallel movement of fourths and fifths often results in non-diatonic lines, particularly within inner voices. Many of the Renaissance works are highly complex in their emphasis on counterpoint and imitation.

3. There is a tendency toward great harmonic freedom. Such devices as parallel movement, altered chords, deliberate dissonances and an increased amount of polyphony or counterpoint all contribute problems of hearing, intonation, independence of chorus sections and general vocal security. Polychordal or polytonal writing may create two simultaneous tonal centers, a problem which often is caused or complicated further by harmonically independent or advanced accompaniments.

4. Rhythmic variations often become highly complex, stressing negation of the bar lines which amateur singers depend upon so heavily. Hemiola effects as well as rapid and frequent changes of meter signature, including the more compound types, may occur. Complex and syncopated rhythmic motives and patterns are used more frequently and are often compounded by contrasting rhythms in some accompaniments or by varying and contrasting rhythms within the vocal parts.

5. Texts are often more complex in their basic literary meanings and polytextual effects appear as a natural result of imitation, counterpoint, and rhythmic variations. An increased number of texts set in Latin, German, French and Italian may be expected. Frequent meter changes, hemiolas and faster tempos may also increase textual problems.

6. The use of multiple tonalities, frequent modulations, semi-nontonal effects and increased chromaticism may contribute to added complexities with regard to key relationships.

7. Generally, tempo limitations are not in evidence and frequent changes of tempo are quite common.

8. There are often great physical demands placed upon singers and accompanist with regard to range, endurance and dynamic shadings, including sudden or frequent contrasts of power versus pianissimo passages.

9. Accompaniment parts range from virtuoso-type demands to extremes of simple, sensitive artistic tenderness, sometimes highly independent, yet often necessarily supportive of the vocal lines.

IV. Original Works

Abt, Franz GS 5992

"Night"

SSA Easy 2 min.

Franz Abt composed chiefly songs (lieder) and part music for men's voices, although he also wrote a few works for female voices, such as this. The work is scored in a predominantly homophonic style, although the middle section is given over to part writing which is independently linear. The chief strength of this work is its lyrical melody, to which the other parts are fittingly subservient. The accompaniment tends to get a little monotonous in its constant reiteration of a broken chord pattern in triplet rhythm; however, a careful accompanist should be able to control this tendency. The range and voice leading throughout are all relatively simple and amateur choirs should experience no difficulty with this work.

Piano c'-g''

Aichinger, Gregor (ed. Clara Tillinghast) W 2899

"Regina Coeli"

SSA Diff. 3 min.

This is a very exciting motet in a fairly fast tempo, and totally contrapuntal throughout. Many of the vocal entrances are imitative and the "pyramiding" of such entrances, strategically delayed by divisions of the measure, adds great excitement to the texture. The vocal lines are conceived in simple diatonic fashion; however, an occasional rhythmic syncopation and the high range of both soprano parts contribute somewhat to the difficulty of the work. There is one minor tempo and meter change about halfway through the work, but this is easily made. The only other tempo changes are an occasional ritardando into a strong cadence in which the moving parts still continue to lend rhythmic drive to the cadences. This is certainly an excellent example of contrapuntal style, strong in appeal and vitality.

Unacc. a-a''

Bach, J. S. ESR 813

"Suscepit Israel"
(from the Magnificat)

SSA Med. -Diff. 2-1/2 min.

This excerpt from Bach's Magnificat in D is scored for only three voices. The music presents a number of difficulties for chorus, yet is worthy of rehearsal time for any women's chorus. Except for the duets which appear in the Cantatas, this and one trio from the motet Jesu Meine Freude are the only works by Bach for women's voices. This trio is entirely polyphonic in style and all three vocal lines are scored in a highly independent manner, usually following an ascending or descending curve. The accompaniment is comprised of repeated pulsating chords which produce a quasi-ostinato effect throughout the work.

Oboe, BC (or piano or organ) g-g''

Barber, Samuel GS 8386

"The Virgin Martyrs" (Op. 8)

SSAA Diff. 3-1/2 min.

This work for women's voices by the American composer Samuel Barber is a very effective number. A high degree of complex syncopation is evident throughout, made more difficult by the lack of accompaniment. Harmonically, the work is quite contemporary in that dissonances are everywhere, though always resolved. The work contains a number of sections in which imitative vocal lines are employed; however, the composer often treats two voices as a unit in contrast to the counterpoint of the other two voices. This makes the work somewhat easier and brings a sense of unity to the structure. Tempo changes, meter changes, key and mood changes abound, all of which contribute to the variety within the work, and add to the excitement engendered within the music.

Unacc. g-ab''

Bartók, Béla Bo Ha 1668

"Don't Leave Me"

SA Easy 1-1/2 min.

This work begins as a two-part canon but deviates from that form following the first sixteen measures. The two vocal lines are predominantly independent; this would serve as a good selection for an amateur chorus to use in an attempt to build independence of sections. The text setting is easy, as are the melody lines. The fourth degree of the scale is raised frequently, thereby creating a modal shift which must be carefully observed.

Unacc. or orchestra b-d''

Bartók, Béla Bo Ha 1670

"Only Tell Me"

SSA Med. 2 min.

This is one of the better works of several which the composer has scored for female voices. The repetition of the theme is a haunting treatment and the harmonies created by the chromatic treatment of the vocal lines are quite interesting. In contrast to many of his other works, which are highly canonic in structure, this music has fewer such passages. The work is not too difficult; however, the vocal parts demand independence of control and good hearing on the part of the singers. The range is very reasonable.

Unacc. or orchestra g-e''

Bell, W. H. Ox 510

"The Flower of Jesse"
(from Four Medieval Songs)

SSA (divisi) Easy-med. 2 min.

This work is a simple setting of a religious song. The harmonies are generally simple and the compositional style is almost entirely homophonic. The accompaniment is predominantly independent of the vocal parts and is also simple in style.

Piano or strings a-a''

Berger, Jean JF 9562

"A Child's Book of Beasts"

SA Easy 6-7 min.

1. The Yak
2. The Polar Bear
3. The Dromedary
4. The Hippopotamus
5. The Rhinoceros
6. The Frog

This is an imaginative group of clever verses set simply but effectively for two-part chorus. The vocal lines are generally easy, but a modern flavor is added by the clever accompaniment, which is cast in a modern idiom. Each selection is scored in duet style except number three, which is a canon. The variation of tempo in the selections provides good contrast when the group is performed as a set. The pieces are especially good to perform before small children. They can be performed by grade school children, providing an excellent early experience in singing music of a contemporary style.

Piano b^b-e''

Brahms, Johannes N 430

"Adoramus"
(We Adore Thee)

SSAA Diff. 2 min.

This motet is number two of a set of three sacred choruses which comprise Op. 37. The harmonies employed in this work make it more difficult than the first and last numbers, which may be due to Brahms' canonic writing in this piece. The first two-thirds of the work is scored in canonic style. The first entrance is between the soprano parts one measure apart, followed by the two alto parts in like manner, although an extra measure separates the paired entrances between sopranos and altos. The final ten measures of the work are in strict homophonic style, with no independent counterpoint. This mixture of styles presents an excellent contrast within the work and exemplifies the versatility of Brahms.

Unacc. g-a''

Broude 136

Brahms, Johannes GS 9115

"Ave Maria" (Op. 12)
("Blessed Are They That Dwell in Thy House")

SSAA Med. 5 min.

This early work by Brahms was probably written during the composer's brief visit to Gottingen in 1858. The text is part of the liturgical invocation to the Virgin Mary. The work is completely homophonic in style and frequent use is made of passages in consecutive thirds (duet-style) for voices in pairs (i. e. two sopranos alternating with two alto parts). Some modulatory passages occur briefly, but the work is predominantly melodic in conception. The accompaniment is quite effective throughout, sometimes doubling the vocal lines, sometimes completely independent of them, as in the "Sancta Maria" section where the voices sing in unison and octave doubling. The work contains a few brief moments of chromatic movement which Brahms so often uses, but it is essentially diatonic and harmonically uncomplex. The original accompaniment is for orchestra.

Orchestra (or piano) g-a''

ECS 2515, P 3651

Brahms, Johannes ECS 2504

"Come Away, Come Away, Death!"
(Komm herbei Tod) (Op. 17, N 2)

SSA Med. 3 min.

This is a unique piece of music based on a text by Shakespeare. (On this point, a performance in English seems perfectly justified.) The work is not difficult, but the accompaniment by two horns and harp is necessary to the effectiveness of the work. The rhythmic motif of the harp is used as a call by which death is summoned. The harp part almost always is used in contrasting phrases or sections against the horns, but almost never with them. The dotted rhythm pattern used by voices, harp and horns is perhaps the most difficult aspect of the work.

Two horns and harp b^b-g''

GS 4301, N. Trios 181

Brahms, Johannes (ed. HC-L) ECS 1069

"Fidelin!" (Op. 44 N. 3)

SSAA (AA) Med. 3 min.

This composition begins with a solo-duet by two alto voices scored in a typical French horn duet manner. This is immediately answered by the chorus on the word "Fidelin", whereupon the two alto soloists take up the next phrase. The answer follows by the full chorus, which remains singing for the remainder of the verse. The text is reminiscent of a "boy meets girl" story, but the musical medium presents the old theme in a fresh and interesting manner. None of the chromatic shifts which are so typical of Brahms are employed in this work; the harmony sounds much like the manner of a harmonized folk song. The accompaniment is quite simple and unobtrusive.

Accomp. g#-f#''

N 335, UPC 72, Kalmus

Brahms, Johannes ECS 1627

"Greetings" (Op. 17 N. 3)
(Der Gärtner - The Gardener)

SSA Med. 4 min.

This is another of the many successful works that Brahms scored for women's voices with harp and horns. This work is not difficult for the vocal or horn parts, although a fairly good harpist is required to give the proper delicateness to the arpeggio figures. The first soprano melody is truly beautiful, and Brahms has let it remain so by not calling any attention to the other voice parts, which are artistically subdued in complexity. This is a love song in all its splendor and the English text by Natalie MacFarren is quite good.

Two horns and harp b^{b}-a^{b}''

N Trios 182, ECS 2503, GS 4302

Brahms, Johannes ECS 494

"I Hear A Harp" (Op. 17 N. 1)
(Es tönt ein voller Harfenklang)

SSA Med. 4 min.

With a good harpist and an average horn player, this is a most effective number despite relatively simple voice parts. There are dissonances in the vocal parts to be sure, but all are excellently prepared and evolved out of the horn accompaniment figure. Long interludes of harp and horn alone provide interesting contrast to the vocal sounds. The range of dynamic contrasts within this piece contributes much to its effectiveness and serves as a good illustration of the Romantic temperament.

Horn and harp d'-g''

N Trios 180, GS 4300

Brahms, Johannes N 429

"O Bone Jesu" (Op. 37 N. 1)

SSA Med. 1-1/2 min.

This sacred work by Brahms, the first of a set of three sacred choruses in his Opus 37, is a Latin motet, not unlike the homophonic motets of Roselli and Palestrina, although the harmonic idiom is quite different. This is a rather striking work in devotional style, but whatever its affinity with the earlier Palestrina manner of writing, there is no mistaking it as Brahms, due largely to the rich nineteenth-century harmonies. The work involves frequent voice crossings and a beautifully scored section of resolving suspensions during the final seven measures which is strongly reminiscent of similar passages in the Requiem.

Unacc. f-g''

Broude 136

Brahms, Johannes 431

"Queen of the Heavens" (Op. 37. N. 3)
(Regina Coeli)

SSAA (SA) Diff. 3-1/2 min.

This is an excellent work written in quite an unusual style for Brahms. The work is much more in the style of Haydn, quite diatonic, with ample florid scale passages. The piece begins with an inverted canonic effect in contrary motion by the two soloists. The chorus joins in a responsorial "Halleluia" which sets the style for a good half of the number. The chorus, however, soon takes up its role of delivering the text and the work ends with both chorus and soloists proclaiming ecstatic "Halleluias".

Unacc. g-g''

Brahms, Johannes (ed. HC-L) ECS 1072

"Roses Are Blooming" (Op. 44 N. 7)
(Rosen in Blüthe)

SSAA Diff. 2-1/2 min.

This piece by Brahms, composed as number seven in a set of twelve lieder and "romanzen", is a typical example of Brahms' writing for women's voices. The tempo marking of allegro is perhaps misleading, as the work should be performed as a lilting waltz. The English words leave much to be desired and the original German text is highly preferable. The harmonic treatment and idiomatic writing are strictly Brahms. Frequent use of chromatic voice leading (and occasional chord shifts) combined with contrasting sections of unison (or octave doubling) melody offer artistic relief and effectively highlight the text. The accompaniment is primarily used in a supportive role.

Piano f#-g#''

JF 4881, Kalmus, P 3669b, UPC 73

Brahms, Johannes 338

"The Nun" (Op. 44 N. 6)
(Die Nonne)

SSAA Med. 3 min.

This is an exceptionally beautiful work, simply and effectively scored. The work is strophic in form and the harmonization and vocal writing are scored accordingly except for the last verse, in which Brahms shifts from minor tonality to major in an extended (or augmented) terce di picardi effect. The accompaniment is indicated ad lib., and the work can certainly be performed without it. However, it is an effective accompaniment and there is no reason to omit it. It is of particular aid in supplying the occasional low sonority often needed in music for women's voices.

Piano ad lib. g-g''

Kalmus, P 3669a

Brahms, Johannes ECS 1055

"Three Love Songs"

SA Med. 3 min.

1. Like The Sunset's Crimson Splendor (Op. 52 N. 4) (Wie des Abends Schöne Röte) 1 min.
2. Bird in Air Will Stray Afar (Op. 52 N. 13) (Völgelein Durch-rauscht die Luft) 1 min.
3. Set Thyself, My Dearest Heart (Op. 65 N. 13) (Mein Geliebter, Setze Dich) 1 min.

These love waltzes are similar in style to the famous Liebeslieder waltzes. None of them is difficult, and the refreshing waltz tempos make them a joy and pleasure to sing. All the duets contain elements of chromaticism, the third being the most difficult. Numbers one and three are not difficult rhythmically, but the second duet includes elements of syncopation which might offer some problems to the amateur choir. All three duets are worthy of serious attention by conductors and are not unduly difficult; however, the accompaniment will require two good pianists.

Piano (4 hands) a#-a^{b}''

UPC 111-112

Brahms, Johannes ECS 1530

"True Lover's Heart" (Op. 66 N. 1)
(Klänge)

SA Med. 2 min.

This is a modestly presented duet which can nevertheless be quite effective when well performed. It is most important that the tempo be not fast, but carefully established to maintain consistency with the text. The rhythm of the voice parts occasionally becomes a little complex and this is the only potential difficulty of the work. There is little non-diatonic chromaticism and no difficult harmonic shifts. This could be considered almost an easy number, except for the slight rhythm problems mentioned and a fairly difficult (and important) piano accompaniment.

Piano d'-g''

Britten, Benjamin Bo Ha

"A Ceremony of Carols" (Op. 23)

SSA (SS) Med. 20 min.

Originally composed for boys' treble voices, this work has come to be a standard part of the repertoire for women's choral groups. The text is in Old English, lending a medieval flavor to the work. This collection of nine carols begins and ends with an early Gregorian melody sung by unison choir and indicated as Processional and Recessional. The accompaniment throughout is for harp, and when the carols are performed as a group (as an extended work) there is a long harp solo (interlude) mid-point in the work. The variations in style, tempos and text of the carols provide effective contrasts. The harmonies are modern, but not particularly difficult. The rhythms are not too difficult, but the solos are more challenging. The writing style employed is essentially of a modern homophonic character; however three of the carols employ canonic imitation. This composition is worthy of almost any amount of rehearsal necessary for a good performance.

Harp (or piano) [expert needed] a^b-a''

Britten, Benjamin

"Old Abram Brown"

SSAA Easy 1-1/2 min.

The effect of this number is that of a round and indeed it is handled in that style for the most part. It is a delightful number, short, but much fun to sing, and the piano accompaniment adds a great deal of interest and contrast to the musical treatment. There is considerable independence of parts when all four vocal sections are busy with the canonic imitation, but it is an easy number to perform.

Piano e'-e''

Buxtehude, Dietrich Bärenreiter-Ausgabe 3625

"Nun Freut Euch Ihr Frommem Mit Mir"
(Cantata)

SS (SS) Easy 12 min.

This is a little-known work of Buxtehude, worthy of the attention of choral directors or voice teachers. It may be performed by a chorus or by two solo voices. When the two vocal lines are interchanged (or inverted) during two brief passages, the work can also be performed by soprano and alto (chorus or soloists). The cantata contains two duets (the opening and closing sections) and two arias, one for soprano I, the other for soprano II. The work begins with an Instrumental Sonata, scored for two violins and basso continuo, and each of the four remaining sections, except the last, closes with an orchestral ritornello. This is a good example of early cantata style. It contains many sections of canonic counterpoint, as well as numerous passages which represent duet-style writing of this early Baroque period.

2 Violins and BC d'-b''

Byrd, William ECS 855

"Rejoice! Rejoice!"

SSAA (A) Diff. 3-1/2 min. total
1-1/2 min. chor. section

This work is divided into two sections, the first being an alto solo with organ or string accompaniment, and set to Francis Kinwelmersh's text "From Virgin pure this day did spring" authored in 1576. The second part of the work is a highly complex polyphonic chorus in four parts, which may be performed alone without the preceding alto solo. When so performed, no accompaniment is used. The alto solo is comprised of long sustained phrases supported by the accompaniment, which is also interspersed between the phrases in the style of the Bach "extended chorales". The chorus section which follows is an exciting contrapuntal composition employing imitative entrances. A change of tempo and meter half-way through begins a new section in a short homophonic passage, followed immediately by a return to the polyphonic style with which the work opened. The counterpoint is complex and the rhythmic phrases across the measures may present some difficulties in early readings.

Organ or string accomp. g-g''
unacc. choral section

Caplet, Andre' Durand

"Messe a Trois Voix"

SSA Diff. 20 min.

This full-length work is in a typical French idiom and contains some fine lyric sections. The long melismatic phrases on occasion are difficult, requiring great vocal control in their execution. Much of the part writing is also difficult and contains a fair degree of chromaticism. In addition to some beautiful moments of melodic writing, there are contrasting dynamic sections which are very exciting. The work abounds in rhythmic, tempo, dynamic and harmonic changes, all of which add great interest to the composition in general. The traditional sections of the mass are included.

Unacc. g-a♭''

Chabrier, Emmanuel BM

"The Shulamite"

SSAA (MS) Diff. 18 min.

This work of extended length by Chabrier is quite modern in its use of tonalities and the vocal lines contain many chromatic passages. In addition, the composer has employed many rhythmic figures which add to the complexity of the composition. There are numerous passages in which triplet figures are preceded or followed by duple figures in the same vocal line. These figures also are used simultaneously in two or more vocal parts. The accompaniment material is no less difficult, nor are the mezzo soprano solo sections, which are also rather extensive. Frequent changes of time signature and tempo also occur throughout the work. The work is a dramatic composition which should be considered only by the most advanced choral groups.

Orchestra (or piano) g-b^{b}''

Couperin, Francois Mercury MC 14

"Troisième Leçon de Ténèbres"
(Lamentation of Jeremiah 1:10-14)

SS (SS) Diff. 10 min.

This is a work worthy of serious consideration by any advanced vocal ensemble. The general framework is that of alternating text assignments between solo voice and the two-part chorus. Some of the solo sections are set in recitative style, others in aria style. The result is a miniature dramatic work of the highest order. The chorus parts are frequently scored in two-part imitative counterpoint and the sequential suspensions which often result are especially effective. Neither the solo sections nor the chorus parts are difficult in themselves; however, the addition of the suggested vocal ornaments adds considerable challenge to those who would consider a more authentic performance. The continuo part is quite traditional, yet often provides a third melodic line to the texture. It cannot be omitted. However, the string parts could be performed by organ, harpsichord or piano.

BC (str. ad lib.) c'-g''

Crichton, Margaret Cur 71762

"Fear No More"

SSA Med. 2-1/2 min.

This is a very worthwhile number which has been neglected in most bibliographic listings. The text is by Shakespeare and the melody is strongly reminiscent of Vaughn Williams or an English folk melody. The work is predominantly homophonic, although it contains a few brief moments of imitative entrances. The whole idiomatic style of the work is that of a folk song.

Unacc. a^{b}-g''

Cui, Cesar Antonovitch (ed. HC-L) BM 715

"Mystic Chorus"
(Chorus Mysticus)

SSA Diff. 5 min.

This work by the famed Russian composer may be considered almost a lament. It is a powerful work which would probably appeal only to more mature choirs and audiences. The vocal parts are highly independent, but not so much in a polyphonic manner, for the work must be regarded as homophonic in style. The work is not too demanding technically; its difficulty lies rather in the profundity of the text and its musical means. The accompaniment is not difficult, but is effective. Some passages in the first part of the work are scored without accompaniment.

Orchestra (or piano) g-a''

Debussy, Claude GS

"The Blessed Damozel"

SSAA (SMS) Med. 20 min.

Following Debussy's winning of the Prix de Rome in 1884 for his cantate L'Enfant Prodigue, he submitted The Blessed Damozel to the Section des Beaux Arts, where it was promptly rejected by the judges for what they termed its unorthodoxy. Actually, the work may be regarded as a masterpiece. Compared with his later works there is little of the unorthodox use of whole-tone and pentatonic scales. The poem by Rossetti is of the highest order, although the English translation does not do justice to Debussy's music. Nevertheless, it is worthy of being performed in either language. The solo sections present more of a challenge than the choral sections, being far more difficult. All of the choral sections are homophonic, and many are scored for unison chorus. The accompaniment is quite difficult and calls for a skillful and sensitive pianist.

Piano f-a''

Dello Joio, Norman GS 9672

"A Jubilant Song"

SSAA (S) Diff. 6 min.

This work, originally composed for mixed voices, has long been one of the best known of Dello Joio's compositions. This setting for women's voices has been arranged by the composer and little if anything has been lost from the original. It is a brilliant and exciting piece of music, not the least significant part of which is the aggressive and driving piano accompaniment, which demands an excellent accompanist. The vocal sections are marked with a great deal of parallel movement in the voices, which are often paired off in alternating passages. The text, adapted from Walt Whitman, is infused with great rhythmic vitality and necessitates frequent shifts of meter. Full rich harmonies are contrasted with frequent sections of unison and octave-doubling sections, while a beautiful cantabile soprano solo (supported by rich choral chords) adds further variety to the work. Tempo and dynamic contrasts are abundant.

Piano g-g#''

Dello Joio, Norman Marks 4307

"Song's End"

SSA Diff. 3-1/2 min.

This work was commissioned by the Women's Glee Club of the State University College at Oneonta, New York on the occasion of the college's Seventy-fifth Anniversary. Dello Joio has scored several passages of poly-tonality and polyrhythm in this setting of the John Payne text. Frequently, there are difficult intervals in the voice parts, and a number of meter changes occur between 4/4, 5/4 and 6/8. The accompaniment is predominantly independent of the vocal lines and employs a generous amount of modern, and sometimes dissonant, chords. Except for one or two brief sections the work is not homophonic, yet it cannot be considered as polyphonic either. The vocal lines maintain a consistent independence throughout, and each is conceived melodically, with only occasional consideration for vertical harmonic results.

Piano b-a''

Des Prés, Josquin WLSM

"Ave Verum"

SSA Easy 1-1/2 min.

There are few easily available works of this early master for women's (or equal) voices. This publication not only makes such a work available, but it is an excellent example of the early Renaissance style of this important composer. The motet begins with the first section scored for SA only, the compositional style being that of imitative counterpoint. This soon changes to a writing style in which the soprano line sings longer melismas over sustained tones in the alto. Near the close of this first section, both parts are scored in a more homophonic style. The second half of the work is in three voice texture, and the writing style is predominantly that of three-part polyphony.

Unacc. f-f''

Destouches, A. G. (Trans. Auguste Chapuis) BM 686

"Shepherd Song"
(Gentils Bergers)

SSA Easy 2 min.

This is a simple treatment of a quite nice lilting melody. The work begins with a "la'la" presentation of the main musical material followed by two verses in strophic-type presentation of the same basic material. An accompaniment by Arthur Ryder has been added, but is not necessary to the performance. The vocal treatment is predominantly homophonic, although the alto part is occasionally treated independently, but simply. The whole nature of the work is much like a folk song.

Accom. a-e''

Diemer, Emm Lou Marks 96

"Fragments from the Mass"

SSAA Med. 6 min.

I Kyrie
II Gloria
III Credo
IV Sanctus
V Agnus Dei

A short mass, in semi-modern idiom, this work contains a considerable degree of variety in the movements. The opening and closing sections employ the same musical material and harmonizations throughout, and are set in a moderately slow tempo with the emphasis on melodic expression. This is true of the Credo section as well. The Gloria and the second part of the Sanctus sections are scored in a more exciting fashion in terms of faster tempos and more rhythmic complexities, and both employ some counterpoint. The Sanctus includes a sustained alto pedal point effect throughout the first half, over which the upper two voices are scored in duet style. The entire work has a modern "flavor" associated with the harmonies. The main performance problems will be found in the rhythmic syncopations which occur in all but one of the sections.

Unacc. g-g''

Duruflé, Maurice Durand

"Tota pulchra es"
(from Coll. Quatre Motets)

SSA (divisi) Med. 2 min.

Based on a Gregorian theme, this is a delightful motet in the contemporary idiom by the French composer Duruflé, who has also scored an excellent Requiem Mass for mixed voices. This motet contains frequent metrical shifts, all easily handled. While much of the musical material is fully composed, the rondo strophic treatment of the original chant is evident and used to good effect. While much of the effect is chordal, each of the parts is treated independently with much interesting material in the inner voices.

Unacc. g-a''

Este, Michael (rev. G. Holst) GS 5359

"How Merrily We Live"

SSA Med. 2 min.

There is excellent vocal training value in singing madrigals, but equally important is that choral groups (especially those of women's voices) find them great fun to sing. This madrigal by Este is an appropriate example of late sixteenth-century madrigal style. It is based on imitation among the three vocal lines, with many passages in which two of the parts are scored in duet fashion. These imitative sections are contrasted with brief moments of pure homophony, and together the two styles provide logical contrasts in style and form. The selection is diatonic and presents no harmonic or rhythmic difficulties; however, independently strong chorus sections are essential for a good performance. The melodic material in all voice parts is highly singable, and the overall result is that the work sounds quite easy.

Unacc. a-f#''

ECS 1062

Fauré, Gabriel (ed. EHG) ESV 860

"Ave Verum"
(Jesu, Word of God Incarnate)

SA | Med. | 2 min.

This is a simple, unpretentious motet in two parts, most of which is alternating phrases and sections between the two voice parts. The vocal phrases are highly melodic, and despite their length, are easily sung. The organ accompaniment is also unpretentious and simply conceived, but in typical Fauré manner, it adds much richness of harmony and color to the effect of the work. A change in tonality from F minor to F major halfway through provides interesting variety to the work, as the accompaniment style also changes at this section.

Organ | a-f''

Fauré, Gabriel | ESV 681

"Tantum Ergo" (Op. 65 N. 2)
(Therefore We Before Him Bending)

SSA (SSA) | Med. | 2-1/2 min.

This work is set in strict homophonic style in the use of both chorus and soloists. The soloists' parts are scored as trio sections, as well as independent solo sections. It is possible to perform the work without the use of soloists by assigning the chorus to these sections. The work begins with a trio for the three soloists, followed by a short two-measure solo pattern being repeated. (There is no solo passage anywhere for the alto solo voice.) The work concludes with an alternating "Amen" section between the trio of soloists and the chorus. The accompaniment role is strictly that of supporting the vocal parts.

Organ | g#-g''

Broude

Gerrish, John | AMP A-295

"A Virgin Most Pure"

SSA (SSA) | Med. | 4 min.

This is an excellent Christmas number which is set in alternating major and minor tonalities and constructed with alternating solo duet and chorus sections, which greatly enhance the beautiful traditional text. The first sporano part is quite easy; however, the two lower parts are filled with difficult interval changes caused by the shifts between major and minor tonality. While the accompaniment is predominantly independent and adds to the effect of the work, it nevertheless supports much of the vocal material, especially in the harmonic sections where such support is needed. In other places, it provides rhythmic contrast which is a welcome addition to the pulsation of the vocal material.

Piano g-e''

Gevaert, François (ed. EHG) ESV 868

"O Filli et Filiae"
(O ye sons and daughters)

SSA Easy-Med. 2 min.

This is a famous text which has been set by many composers. Gavaert has assigned the first three verses to each of the three vocal sections as solo passages, with the "Alleluia" refrain being scored for full chorus between each of the three verses. Each of the three solo assignments is set to a different melody, with the only repeated material being the "Alleluia". The final verse begins with unison chorus and employs the first melody for its text. The "Alleluia" section is used again to close out the work. Diatonic throughout, the work's only difficult aspect is the rhythmic syncopation presented in each of the four verses.

Unacc. a-f''

Gibbs, C. Armstrong Ox 2230

"O, Praise God in His Holiness"
(Psalm CL)

SA Med. 2-1/2 min.

This is a stirring and very impressive anthem which the composer wrote especially for the 1953 Festival of the Federation of Essex (England) Women's Institutes in honor of Queen Elizabeth II's coronation. The work begins on a five-note theme in the accompaniment, which is taken up by the choir in unison, and which returns in various keys throughout the work. The scoring contains much unison, as well as excellent part writing in which extremes of power are contrasted with pure melodic lyricism. The accompaniment is quite independent and dramatic throughout the work, and dynamic contrasts both in accompaniment and chorus parts are plentiful and well handled.

Piano, organ or orchestra c'-g''

Haines, Edmund Broude

"Dialogue from the Book of Job"
(In Memoriam November 22, 1963)

SSAA (SA) Diff. 8 min.

This composition was commissioned by Harold Aks and the Sarah Lawrence Chorus in memory of President John F. Kennedy. Haines is a member of the faculty at Sarah Lawrence College and has been a recipient of a Pulitzer Prize and two Guggenheim Fellowships. This is an extremely difficult work, mainly due to the large amount of dissonant effects created in the vocal parts and also in the accompaniment. More acute is the problem of large, angular intervals within each vocal line, and extremes of ranges which the composer scores. Difficult rhythms and disjunct melismas occur frequently in the vocal lines. The accompaniment is usually independent of the vocal line, and is frequently treated as another ensemble which contrasts with the vocal sections. The work also contains several sections for speaking chorus against solo passages.

Piano f-b''

Handel, Georg Friedrich (ed. HC-L) ESC 1039

"O Lovely Peace, with Plenty Crowned"
(from Judas Maccabaeus)

SA Med. 3 min.

This pastoral-type duet is a fine example of two-part writing in the late Baroque period. The piano accompaniment establishes both the mood and the musical material for the vocal writing which follows. The vocal material begins with a long statement by the soprano alone, followed by a similar length section by the alto voice, using the same text. The two voices then take up the lovely duet material which forms most of the remainder of the work. A closing ritornello by the piano rounds off the selection in the traditional Baroque aria pattern.

Piano c'-f''

Handel, Georg Friedrich Cur 70841

"Come Ever Smiling Liberty"
(from Judas Maccabaeus)

SS Easy 1-1/2 min.
or SA

This is a simple duet from Handel's Oratorio Judas Maccabaeus that is delightful and interesting to sing. The work begins with a canonic imitation between the two voice parts, which is then resolved into typical Baroque duet-style writing. There are a number of short sequentially treated phrases between the two voice parts which give the piece interest from the standpoint of independence within each voice part; simple but effective. The accompaniment is not difficult, but must be performed with clarity and knowledge of the "thorough-bass" style.

Accomp. d'-e''

N School 21

Handel, Georg Friedrich GS 150

"The Smiling Dawn"
(from Jeptha)

SSA Med. 3 min.

This chorus from Handel's Oratorio Jeptha is in typical Handelian fashion, employing homophony and sprinkled with occasional phrases of polyphonic imitation. The Bouree-type tempo gives the work a lilting joyousness which adequately captures the gaiety and lightness of the text. There are several sections in which the composer scores a florid sequential melody to a single syllable, usually in one voice part at a time. There are also a number of phrase sections in which two paired voices are featured while the third voice is temporarily unscored. As in the case of the vocal parts, the accompaniment is quite simple and is used mainly to support and double the voice parts.

Piano (orig. orch.) a-g''

Handl (Gallus), Jacob (ed. P. Boepple) Mercury DCS 31

"Replenti Sunt Omnes"

SSAA-SSAA Easy-Med. 1-1/2 min.
(double choir)

This is a fine example of the double choir work for which Handl has become so well known. It is scored for two choirs of equal voices in predominantly homophonic style. The two choirs alternate brief choral passages, usually repeating the text just previously sung. Overlapping of these sections is effectively achieved by having one of the choirs begin a new section while the opposite choir is just completing a phrase.

There are no difficult rhythms, no meter changes. The chord progressions are all diatonic in a minor tonality (except the final "terce di picardy" chord). This would be a reasonably easy introduction to antiphonal choir singing, an experience which is quite exciting to the amateur singer.

Unacc. f-a''

Harris, Roy GS 8503

"Whitman Triptych"

SSSSA 1. "I Hear America Singing" 2 min.
SSA 2. "An Evening Lull" 1 min.
SSAA 3. "America" 2-1/2 min.

Diff.

These works by Harris are quite different from the usual choral music to be found. The first number for example has no text, but simply an alternating of "oh" and "ah". At least half of the selection is nothing more than an alternating among the four soprano parts of phrases set in unison, although cleverly scored in a smooth "hocketing" fashion. The second number contains a considerable amount of dissonance, much of it unresolved, but employing text throughout. A slight change of tempo is also included. The third selection begins with the "oh" - "ah" alternation of the first number, but the text is soon introduced. This number is comprised of both homophony and counterpoint and is the most difficult of the three, as the four parts are quite independent. Several tempo, meter, and mood changes endow this with considerably more variety than the preceding numbers of the set.

Unacc. g-a''

Hasse, Johann Adolf (ed. Hugo Leichtentritt) GS

"Miserere"
(Psalm LI)

SSAA (SAA) Diff. 20 min.

Known primarily as a composer of operas, Hasse was one of the musical celebrities of the eighteenth century. The Miserere was written in 1728 for the girls' chorus and ensemble of the Conservatorio degl' Incurabili, an orphan asylum and hospital in Venice. The work is comprised of six major sections: three for chorus, two for soprano solo and one for alto duet. The choral sections are a mixture of homophony and polyphony with passages in two-part duet style in each of the chorus sections. The solo and duet sections are much in the style of the solos and duets of the Bach Cantatas or Handel Oratorios. The orchestral material (or piano accompaniment) is generally quite independent of the vocal material in the treatment of the melodic portions, although it is supportive of the harmonies in the choral sections.

Strings or piano g-g''

Hodge, Talbot Ch 6712

"Cuckoo Song"

SS Med. 2 min.

This work is quite impressive and generally simple to perform. Both the accompaniment and the echoing between the two voice parts contribute to the traditional "cuckoo" concept of musical settings dealing with this favorite musical bird. There are, of course, sections with considerable independence of parts, but this is artistically contrasted with a reasonable amount of two-part harmonic writing. An occasional shift from 4/4 to 3/4 meter wisely avoids rhythmic monotony. Except for a few intervals which may be a little difficult to hear on first readings, this is a relatively simple piece.

Accomp. c'-f#''

Holst, G. Cur 8792

"A Dream of Christmas"

SA Easy 3 min.

This simple setting by Holst of Mary Segar's beautiful text from her "Medieval Anthology" is a significantly unusual number. The melodic pattern is in Dorian mode for the first half of the selection, and this is most effective in capturing the beauty of the text. Much of this selection is in unison, although the refrain-like section is scored in simple two-part writing following each of five short verses. The accompaniment is quite simple and serves only to reinforce and support the vocal line, although it does contribute significantly to the modal harmonies. Both the text and the modality employed contribute to making this an exceptionally fine Christmas number which is refreshingly different. The basic structure is that of two three-measure phrases followed by two four-measure phrases.

Accomp. d'-d''

Holst, Gustave Gray 312

"Ave Maria"

SSAA-SSAA (double chorus) Med. 4-1/2 min.

This is a motet composed for double chorus, which the composer dedicated to the memory of his mother. The work is in slow tempo and homophonic style, but is difficult because of its wide range and the difficult interval skips which often occur within the inner voices. Much of the vocal movement is of a scale nature, which results in sections of rich harmony and poignant dissonances. The work is unaccompanied and as a result, there is an excellent interplay between the two choruses, which Holst treats equally in importance. This should be a very challenging work for the more mature choir.

Unacc. f-bb''

Holst, Gustave Gray 286

(from Choral Hymns from the Rig Veda)
Group II
No. 3 "Funeral Chant" (Op. 26)

SSSAAA Med. 3 min.

This third number in the second group of Holst's Opus 26 is a most unique selection. The work is based entirely on an eight-note chant, which the composer treats very effectively. With the devices of parallelism, canonic imitation, fragmentation and augmentation, he has created a most impressive piece of music. The accompaniment also employs the chant theme modestly, and in addition creates a sustained descending scale passage in the bass which is very effective. The difficulties of performance are centered in the medieval-type parallelism which constitutes the main portion of the work and in the canonic entrances of the divisi voice parts.

Piano g-g''

Holst, G. APS 421

"Four Old English Carols"

SSAA (SA) Med. 1-1/2 min. each

1. A Babe is born

2. Now let us sing
3. Jesus, thou the virgin-born (no accompaniment)
4. In Bethlehem, that noble place

Each of these four choral carols by the English master is fresh and unhackneyed. Some hint of modal flavor appears in each of the carols, and the words are mainly from the fifteenth century. Piano accompaniment is featured in numbers two and four and lends exceptional importance to the harmonies of the carols. (Number four is scored for unison voice.) Contrasts of tempo, line signature, rhythm and key make the set an interesting unit to be performed as a group, although each is sufficient to be performed alone. Of Swedish origin, but born in England, Holst has completely adapted himself to the English style of composition, as these carols clearly testify.

Accomp. a^b-e^{b}''

Holst, G. SB 1988

"Hecuba's Lament" (Op. 31 N. 1)
(from the Trojan Women of Euripides)

SSAA (SMS or A) Diff. 10 min.

This is a very difficult, unusual work for women's voices. In addition to the chorus parts which alternate between full harmony and many unison passages, the work calls for a soprano soloist and a mezzo soprano (or alto) soloist in the lead role who possesses an excellent range (g-f''). This perhaps is the main cause of the work's neglect. While it is possible to perform the work with piano alone, it is more effective when accompanied by orchestra. The voice parts, while not too difficult harmonically, contain difficult rhythms and time signatures, which are often unfamiliar (and hence, uncertain) to amateur singers. The work requires an excellent accompanist, but nevertheless is worthy of serious consideration by advanced choirs.

Orch, or piano & str. quintet
(or piano alone)

Holst, G. SB 1633

"Hymn to Dionysus"
(from The Bacche of Euripides) (Op. 31 N. 2)

SSAA Diff. 12 min.

This work is even more difficult than Op. 31 N. 2 ("Hecuba's Lament") and really demands a virtuoso choral group. After a sixteen-measure orchestral introduction, the chorus begins a long section of highly syncopated unison singing. There are a few brief returns to unison scoring, but for the most part the scoring is in parts, quite difficult and interesting in their dissonant treatment. Frequent tempo and meter changes are common in this work, as is constant syncopation which produces interesting and difficult rhythms. The accompaniment is scored for orchestra, but may be performed with either piano and string quintet or piano alone, with obvious reduced effect.

Orch. or piano & str. quintet (or piano alone) — a-b^{b}''

Holst, Gustave — N 514

"Love on My Heart from Heaven Fell" (Op. 44 N. 6)

SSSA (S) — Med. — 2 min.

This work, one of seven part songs in Holst's Op. 44, is perhaps more difficult than it appears, but should not be too hard for the average choir. The text by Robert Bridges is set artistically by Holst, somewhat in a folk song style. The work begins with a soprano solo, the melody of which is then taken up by the choir in imitative treatment, prior to a homophonic section in which the voice parts move quite independently. A short interlude for strings precedes a unison section for chorus which, except for one measure in harmony, closes the statement of the vocal phrase by strings. This is worthwhile, and not too difficult a selection.

Strings or piano — a-g''

Hovhaness, Alan — AMP A-277

"Ave Maria" (from Triptych)

SSAA — Med. — 3 min.

The abbreviated traditional text is set in a not-too-difficult modern idiom, the effect of which is enhanced considerably by the original instrumental scoring. Following a five-measure instrumental introduction, the four voices take up the text "Ave Maria" in a modern homophonic style of chordal changes, with an occasional melismatic line in the first soprano. No other words are sung, only "Ave Maria". At measure twenty-five, the texture shifts to a polyphonic imitative counterpoint. For a brief episode following, three of the four voices employ melismas before the choral parts return to the opening homophonic style. The accompaniment is largely doubling of the vocal lines or sustained chords which create interesting tonal colors. The closing section is made up of long sustained chords beneath a melismatic soprano line. Simple shifts between 3/2 and 2/2 meter are used throughout.

2 Oboes, 2 horns & harp (or 2 trumpets, 2 trombones & piano) g-a''

Ingegneri, Marc Antonio ECS 1506

"Vere Languores Nostros"
(Surely He hath borne our griefs)

SSA Med. 1 min.

This is an exceptionally short Latin motet; a very beautiful example of sixteenth-century fusion of homophonic and polyphonic style. Ingegneri was choirmaster at the Cathedral at Cremona, where he had the great distinction of having the now-celebrated Claudio Monteverdi as his pupil. For many years, his works were ascribed erroneously to Palestrina, including this Responsorium (motet). This work is delicate and simple in its vocal lines; however, its contrapuntal nature and flowing melodic curves need a mature approach to performance.

Unacc. a^b-e^{b}''

Kodály, Zoltán Bo Ha 1711

"Ave Maria"

SSA Med. 2 min.

Many settings of this familiar text exist for all types of vocal combinations, but surely none is more effective than this modern setting by Kodály. The first part of the work is scored for alto voice in an almost chant-like intoning of the familiar text, while the upper two voices enter in an echo effect at the end of each phrase with the words "Ave Maria". The latter sections of the work employ a different technique. Here the upper voices begin in duet fashion, while the lower voice continues independently. The closing section of the work begins with an independence of vocal lines, sometimes imitative in style. The dissonances and harmonies are quite rich in the second half of the piece and the overall effect is highly impressive.

Unacc. g-g''

Kodály, Zoltán Bo Ha 1890

"Cease Your Bitter Weeping"

SSA (divisi) Med. 4-1/2 min.

Based on a religious song or hymn, this has been set most effectively by Kodály. Each vocal line, while contributing to some unusual harmony effects, is treated almost totally as a melody. Frequent changes of meter are employed to give the most natural pulse to the text. These are not difficult changes, and recur in a sequence pattern so that they actually become easy. The text is the weakest aspect of the work, in that the syncopations originally scored by the composer do not always coincide with the translated text. There are some excellent dynamic contrasts built into the selection, and the added differentiations between syncopation and sostenuto sections are artfully placed. The harmonies are not unduly difficult, although there is frequent shifting of modal patterns both melodically and harmonically.

Unacc. d-g''

Kodály, Zoltán (ed. WGW) Ox 550

"King Ladislaus' Men"
(Magyars and Germans)

SSAA Diff. 4 min.

This is a rather unusual work, being based on Hungarian traditional rhythms and melodic fragments which the composer has combined in an exciting way. The work is scored in dialogue form as if between the Magyar people and the German people--a debate about a bridge. The English text is given, and undoubtedly lends humorous understanding to the work, but the music is far more rich and exciting when sung in the original text. The work is full of syncopated rhythmic motives, which are not easy, but the melodic patterns are essentially only two. They are combined in rhythmic, parallel and contrapuntal ways to produce a sensation of great complexity. Tempo and mood changes provide considerable variety.

Unacc. g-ab''

Kodály, Zoltán (ed. WGW) Ox 541

"The Deaf Boatman"

SSA Easy 1-1/2 min.

This is a humorous song based on a popular Hungarian text. The work is scored in such a way that practically any choir can perform it easily. There are a few sections of parallel fifths and, except for the last few measures, the rest of the work is scored in unison, or major thirds. The text is a purported conversation between a boatman and his boat. The work is quite diatonic and therefore easy to sing. Some aspects of syncopation in the rhythm might cause amateur choirs some slight difficulties during first readings.

Unacc. g-f#''

Lasso, Orlando di Bank #2

"Adoramus Te"

SSA Easy-Med. 1 min.

Of the many settings of this text, this version by di Lasso is one of the simplest. A reasonable amount of homophonic style is included, so that the work is comprised of a mixture of imitative and chordal styles. This setting contains no melodic or harmonic problems; however, the few melismas contain some rhythmic variation. A few fleeting suggestions of easy key change identify the work as being slightly modal. These modality changes are minor and untroublesome, yet present an interesting harmonic variety within the selection.

Unacc. b^b-g''

Lasso, Orlando di (ed. EHG) ESV 890

"Adoramus Te Christe"
("We Adore Thee, O Lord")
(from Magnum Opus Musicum No. 177)

SSSAA Diff. 1-1/2 min.

Di Lasso set this text to music on several different occasions, but this setting is the most complex and masterful. Considerable crossing of voices is characteristic. The constant overlapping of phrases resulting from masterful counterpoint provides an excellent example of the high degree of development which the polyphonic style had achieved during this period, especially in the hands of this great tonal master. With its intricate polyphonic web and frequent shifting between major and minor tonalities, this is an exceptionally beautiful expression of reverence.

Unacc. a-f''

Lasso, Orlando di (ed. Paul Boepple) Mercury MC 11

"Cantiones Duarum Vocum"
(Magnum Opus I-XX)

SS (or SA) Med. 1-2 min. each

Twelve Motets for Two Equal Voices

1. Beatus Vir
2. Beatus Homo
3. Oculos Non Vidit
4. Justus Cor Suum Tradet
5. Exspectatio Justorum
6. Qui Sequitur Me
7. Justi Tulerunt Spolia
8. Sancti Mei
9. Qui Vult Venire
10. Serve Bone
11. Fulgebunt Justi
12. Sicut Rosa

These famous motets for two voices are among 24 such compositions which the composer scored. The other 12 are textless and presumably for instruments. These are all excellent examples of two-part counterpoint, often of the imitative type, but often including less strict contrapuntal technique. Each is a complete work in itself and may be considered for performance as such. Rhythmically, the motets are complex due to constant overlapping of phrases and oft-changing motifs. These motets are excellent material for training a chorus in singing independent vocal lines and developing rhythmic security. They are also musically worthwhile.

Unacc. g-g''

Lasso, Orlando di Bank #21

"Hodie Apparuit"

SSA Easy 1 min.

This is a relatively easy example of imitative polyphony of sixteenth-century style for three equal voices. The work presents no difficulties of harmonic or rhythmic elements. A few short melismas occur; however, they are diatonic and set at a moderate tempo. The three vocal lines are all quite interesting melodically, with the short thematic material of a rising fourth followed by three descending notes appearing in each voice, somewhat as a "motto" theme. This work would provide a conductor of a less-experienced choir or glee club an excellent opportunity to introduce his singers to polyphonic style within their performance abilities.

Unacc. g-g''

ECS 1285, JF 6438

Lasso, Orlando di (ed. Paul Boepple) Mercury DCS 21

"Three Psalms"
(on Texts and Tunes from Caspar Ulenberg's Psalter)

SSA Diff. 1 min. each

1. Psalm 25, Judica Me Domine
2. Psalm 5, Verba Mea Auribus
3. Psalm 43, Veus, Auribus Nostris

These three psalms originally appeared in a collection of 53 psalms, half of which were by Lasso, the other half by his son. Lasso has used Protestant tunes from Ulenberg's Psalter (1582) as cantus firmi in these settings. All three of the psalms are highly polyphonic in style, and some of the diatonic scale passages are difficult to perform, mainly because of their rhythmic complexity. Number two is perhaps the easiest, although all three compositions make demands on alto range and vocal control of all choir sections. This edition uses no bar lines, which helps proper text accentuation but presents more difficult reading problems to the amateur choir.

Unacc. f-g''

Lawes, William (ed. WGW) Ox JP 4

"Gather Your Rosebuds"
(adapted)

SSA Med. 2-1/2 min.

This work is from John Playford's *Musical Companion*, first published in 1667. It was used originally by a London musical club of which Playford was a member. This work, with its famous text by Herrick, is very much in the homophonic style of the early seventeenth century. The work contains an occasional shift of meter to accommodate the text, and crossing of the two highest voices appears throughout, though resulting in no problems of performance.

Unacc. a^{b}-f''

Lawes, William (ed. WGW) Ox JP xll

"Come Lovely Chloris"

SSA Med. 2-1/2 min.

This work is clearly homophonic and illustrates the musical style changes which were taking place at the beginning of the seventeenth century. The vocal parts are not difficult and the work is firmly tonal. There is some crossing of voices which involves the second soprano part in the higher register, but otherwise no problems occur as a result of the crossing of such parts. The text is very good and typical of the love ballads so popular during this period. A rehearsal piano part is given, but in all likelihood the work was performed originally with harpsichord continuo.

Unacc. g-a''

Lawes, William (ed. WGW) Ox JP X1

"O My Clarissa"

SSA Easy 2 min.

The tempo marking of Allegretto keeps this piece in a light vein, although certainly the text, typical of the English love ballads, is serious. Voice crossings occur, but they do not create any performing problems. This work is easier than most others in the Playford Collection. The use of the minor key involves the lowered sixth degree contrasted with the raised seventh degree, but this should present no problems.

Unacc. g-g''

Liszt, Franz GS 4392

"O Filli et Filiae"
(Easter Hymn)
(from Oratorio Christus)

SAA Easy 2 min.

This is a simple setting of the popular "O Filii" text, which has been set by a number of composers. The work is based on a modal melody (Dorian mode) and therein lies its charm. This setting, as are most settings of this text, is in strophic form. Each subsequent verse employs the same melodic material, with an Alleluia "refrain" preceding the work and closing it. The accompaniment is for Harmonium, a small reed type instrument which was popular in the nineteenth century, but a regular organ could undoubtedly serve as a substitute. The accompaniment does little more than double the voice parts (except in the final cadence in which it has sole responsibility for establishing the terce di picardi chord) and it could probably be excluded from a performance of the work.

Harmonium (or organ) c'-c''

Liszt, Franz BM

"The 137th Psalm"

SSAA (S) Easy 12-15 min.

The text of this extended work by Liszt is one which has attracted many composers. ("By the rivers of Babylon, there we sat down, yea, we wept".) The opening material of this cantata is scored for soprano solo, violin obbligato and accompaniment in a style which the editors term "mournful and mystical". The solo material is not difficult in this section, nor in the sections which follow. The remaining vocal material is comprised of solo sections and choral sections of long phrases which alternate on the word "Jerusalem". The only text sung by the chorus is the word "Jerusalem". This work is quite simple and involves no technical demands on the chorus singers except those associated with producing good tone quality and pitch accurateness in soft passages.

Violin, harp, piano and organ or Harmonium a^b-f''

Lotti, Antonio (ed. HC-L) ECS 1845

"Mass" (in B^b)

SSA Med. 30 min.

This mass, also available for men's voices, is written in sixteenth-century polyphonic style, although composed in the early eighteenth century. It is highly contrapuntal, and imitative counterpoint is common throughout. Part of the difficulty of this work rests on the fact that there is a great deal of singing by all voice parts, with practically no rests. Also, the soprano range seems consistently high for an amateur group and this could cause tiring and pitch-slipping. Despite the emphasis on polyphony, the voice parts are quite natural in their voice leadings and melodic treatment. There are some excellent sections of falling suspensions, which can be exquisite when sung sensitively.

Unacc. g-g''

Lubeck, Vincent Con 97-6379

"Christmas Cantata"

SS (or SA) Easy 10 min.

This is an unpretentious, but expressive composition which has been fashioned most sensitively in the Baroque Cantata tradition. An instrumental sonata serves as an introduction to the vocal sections, which are comprised of three duets and two solos, all rather brief. The instrumental accompaniment is employed throughout the composition, with the two violins scored in duet style and often alternating passages with the vocal duet. This cantata is not dramatic in the sense of contrasting tempos, rhythms or dynamics. Its dramatic impact lies rather in the text, and the expressive shadings and subtle beauties of the vocal lines in combination with the instrumental accompaniment. The range is simple, the vocal lines and harmonies are all diatonic, and even the instrumental accompaniment is reasonably simple.

2 violins, cello (or bass) and keyboard — f'-f''

<u>Martini, Giambattista</u> — SB 1824

"A Measure to Pleasure Your Leisure"
(with Rhymes That Are Witty and Pretty)

SSA — Med. — 1-1/2 min.

This is a delightful glee of the early eighteenth century. All the parts are great fun to sing and the listener is sure to share in the jollity. The voice parts are imitative in some places, but for the most part the piece is scored as a duet for soprano parts, with the alto line being complementary, but highly independent. There are no difficult harmonic sections, nor are there any difficult rhythmic sections. While the tempo is marked fast, the text implies an occasional change of tempo which adds some variety to the work.

Unacc. — g-g''

<u>Martini, Giambattista</u> — Bank #24

"Tristes Est"

SSA — Easy-Med. — 1 min.

This is a very simple, lovely motet in predominantly homophonic style. The work contains a few brief passages which contain elements of imitative counterpoint, but these are usually scored as a single voice against two others which are performing in duet style. The work contains no difficult rhythm or harmonic elements. As in the case of a number of other publications from this series (Bank), this would be a good work for amateur choirs to perform as an early experience in singing music of this period.

Unacc. g-f''

Martinu, Bohuslav Bo Ha 1945

"The Birth of Our Lord"
(Narozeni Pane)

SSA (divisi) Med. 2 min.

A rather unusual setting of a unique text, this work describes the circumstances of Christ's birth in an original way. Each phrase length is different in length. The vocal parts are fairly rhythmic, with the violin part establishing an almost "drone-like" effect, sometimes doubled in one of the voices. Rhythmic and melodic patterns are often repeated in short phrases, both in vocal lines and in the accompaniment. The accompaniment eventually becomes independent of the vocal parts and takes on a more melodic role. A contrasting lyric-type section occurs in the vocal parts prior to a repetitive ending. The original Bohemian text is included with an English translation by Nancy Bush.

Violin b^b-g''

Mechem, Kirche ECS 2561

"I Shall Not Care"

SSAA Diff. 2 min.

This is a modern setting of a poem by Sara Teasdale. The composer has produced a fairly large number of dissonant sounds through the use of logical and melodic linear movement between the voice parts. The work contains a variety of simple rhythmic effects which prevent any monotonous use of quarter note and half note patterns. Dynamic contrasts are strategically placed to highlight the text, although the work is not a dynamic or dramatic piece. This is an unpretentious composition, but one which contains many subleties and nuances of expression. The rating of "difficult" is assigned solely on the basis of the harmonic effects created between voices; otherwise, it is a work of only medium difficulty.

Unacc. a-f#''

Mendelssohn, Felix GS 5853

"I Would That My Love"

SS Easy 3 min.

This is a very lovely, simple two-part chorus written in duet style throughout. The style of composition is very much like that of the early romantic lieder, and the work contains a free flowing melody which is charming. The text, by the great German poet Heine, deals with romantic allusions to the subject of love. The range is reasonable and, except for an occasional chromatic linear progression, the work is quite diatonic and simple. Contrast is achieved in one small phrase section by scoring the voices in unison. Additional contrast is achieved in the piano accompaniment, which, in typical romantic style, is very important to the overall effect. This is a work which can be handled easily by any choir with good results.

Accomp. c#'-f#''

Mendelssohn, Felix ECS 1839

"Ye Sons of Israel" (Op. 39 N. 2)
(Laudate Pueri)

SSA Med. 4-1/2 min.

This is a very stirring setting in paraphrase of Psalm 113:1, 2. The work is highly diatonic, not at all in the romantic style of the composer's day. The vocal parts contain a considerable degree of imitative devices; however, much of the work is homophonic in style. The accompaniment is designed chiefly to support the vocal parts, although it is quite florid. The work is quite fully scored throughout and tends to be rather powerful, both as a result of the full scoring and the style of vocal writing. The vocal lines are not difficult and the intervals are all reasonable.

Organ or piano b^b-g''

Milhaud, Darius Mercury MC 189

"Cantata From Proverbs"

SSA Diff. 9-1/2 min.

This work is divided into three sections as follows:

1. Who Crieth "Woe"? (Proverbs XXIII:29-35)
2. The Woman Folly (Proverbs IX:13-18)
3. A Woman of Valor (Proverbs XXXI:10-31)

They may be performed separately or as a group. Rhythmic syncopation is one of the chief characteristics of the work, and this feature gives the work a high degree of vitality and interest. A polyrhythmic treatment of the three vocal lines is the result of the imitative treatment of the text, although a homophonic-type text treatment occurs frequently. The difficulty in this work may be attributed to the melodic intervals employed. They often result in modern-type chords, but the harmonies are not essentially difficult or dissonant. The accompaniment in each of the three sections is independent and offers little harmonic or melodic support to the vocal lines. Nevertheless, the effects produced by the accompaniment are stunning and contribute significantly to the overall effect of the work. A keyboard instrument may be used if necessary.

Harp, oboe, cello f#-a''

Miller, C. E. GS 8515

"Come Away, Sweet Love, and Play Thee"

SSA Med. 2 min.

This is a delightful ballet madrigal by the eighteenth-century English composer, complete with "fa-la" sections. It is scored with almost complete independence of parts, which shows that contrapuntal writing certainly did not die out in the seventeenth century. The vocal parts are not difficult, although there is frequent crossing of vocal lines among all voice parts. The contrapuntal style of the piece is interrupted halfway through by a few brief homophonic sections, which alternate with polyphony. This is an exceptionally effective madrigal.

Unacc. b^b-g''

Miller, C. E. Cur 71530

"I Saw Lovely Phyllis"

SSA Med. 3 min.

This is another exceptionally good choral work by Miller, but one which, judging by the text, has been adapted for women's voices by the composer. Its composition style is considerably more homophonic, with occasional phrases in unison. The "fa-la" sections are more independent, in the style of "Bach-type" resolving suspensions. While the text is not well suited to women (the words are obviously those of a young man), the music is so charming that it hardly seems fair to eliminate the song for this reason. A program note explaining its musical worth and historic stylistic significance would justify its use by a women's choir.

Unacc. a-f#''

Miller, C. E. Cur 71512

"Welcome, Sweet Pleasure"

SSA Med. 2 min.

This is another excellent ballet madrigal by the little-known English composer, Miller. The work is basically homophonic, although there is considerable madrigal-type counterpoint throughout, especially in the "fa-la" refrain. The work has three verses, all set to the same music and each ending with the "fa-la" refrain. This is not a difficult work despite its counterpoint, and all the vocal lines are interesting to sing.

Unacc. a-f#''

Monteverdi, Claudio (ed. Paul Boepple) Mercury MC 24

"Sacrae Cantiunculae"
Nos. 12 & 16

SSA Med.

1. Angelus Ad Pastores Ait 1 min.
2. Hodie Christus Natus Est 1-1/2 min.

These two works, number 12 and number 16 of the 22 selections comprising the Sacrae Cantiunculae, were published when Monteverdi was only fifteen years old. Monteverdi, even at this early age, possessed a mature knowledge of the polyphonic style of his time. There are passages of imitative counterpoint included, but much of the counterpoint is less strict, yet no less impressive. Both of these works are for the Christmas season, but could be performed at any time using the Latin text. They present no major performance problems regarding rhythm or harmonic idiom and, compared with many works of this same period, are relatively easy, except for the overlapping of phrases. The first selection has two meter changes, from duple to triple meter and a return to duple meter.

Unacc. f-g''

Morley, Thomas ECS 283

"See! Lovely Day is Dawning"

SA Med. 1-1/2 min.

This appears to be in its original form, in only

two voice parts. This work is not difficult, although as happens often with madrigals, there is almost complete independence of parts. The work contains a degree of imitation between the two parts. There is a meter change partway through, which affords a nice rhythmic contrast. The original common meter returns, before a final change to triple meter at the conclusion.

Unacc. b-e''

Nelson, Ron Summy 5052

"Jehovah, Hear Our Prayer"

SSAA (S) Med. Diff. 2-1/2 min.

Ron Nelson is a graduate of the Eastman School of Music and served for some time as assistant professor of music at Brown University and as director of the Pembroke College Glee Club. The text is based on selections from Psalms 13 and 22 and is a prayerful supplication to God. The work begins with a chant-like melody sung in unaccompanied unison. The same material is also used to close the work. In between, Nelson has scored a finely wrought series of tonal prayers, often in unisons, parallels, chant-effects and contemporary progressions which achieve a stunning effect. Frequent changes of meter occur and the work is enhanced further by an imaginative accompaniment which is wholly independent. This is an exceptionally fine and effective choral number and is not too difficult.

Piano a-b#''

Palestrina, G. P. GS 6251

"Ave Maria"

SSSA Diff. 3 min.

This motet, based upon the familiar Gregorian plain chant, is somewhat more complex than many of Palestrina's works; however, it does contain some sections which are paired off for two or three voices in brief homophonic sections. Imitation is an important basis of vocal line development and frequent chromatic alterations occur in the three lower parts. The first half of the work contains the somewhat unusual feature of the original Gregorian chant being stated in the alto line, while above, the three soprano parts weave a contrapuntal web out of the first phrase of that chant, freely treated. The range is fairly demanding of the three soprano parts.

This factor contributes to the difficulty of the work.

Unacc. a-f#''

Palestrina, G. P. (ed. GWW) GS 9814

"Benedictus"
(from Mass O Admirabile Commercium)

SSAA Med.-Diff. 3 min.

The mass O Admirabile Commercium takes its name from the Christmas motet, and the composer made two complete mass settings based on the motet. (One for five voices, and one for eight-part double chorus.) The "Benedictus" setting is a somewhat slow-moving treatment of the text and provides an excellent example of the imitative, contrapuntal style and the "classical" use of overlapping phrases. There are a few short sections in homophonic style, but the majority of the work treats the voice parts in an independent, though interdependent manner. The dissonances created by suspensions are typical of sixteenth-century style, and the long, luring melodic lines in each of the four voice parts are largely diatonic, thus creating no modal change problems. There are no complexities in either rhythm or harmony. The work is a traditional presentation of polyphonic inter-weaving texture.

Unacc. f-g''

Palestrina, G. P. GS 258

"Crucifixus"
(from Mass Assumpta est Maria)

SSA Med. 1-1/2 min.

This excellent setting is a fine example of the sixteenth-century polyphonic style of vocal writing. The vocal parts are often paired off in alternating sections; however, a third voice is usually employed contrapuntally in such sections. There is a sufficient degree of homophonic sections which testify to Palestrina's more conservative nature. Imitation, especially at points of voice entries, is quite common and overlapping of phrases, traditional in sixteenth-century polyphonic style, is commonly featured. The work is highly diatonic, with no modal shifts employed, although temporary modulations to the key of the supertonic do occur.

Unacc. g-f''

Palestrina, G. P. GS 5605

"Innocentes pro Christo"

SSAA Diff. 2-1/2 min.

This motet by Palestrina is polyphonic throughout, and the complete independence of vocal lines, based heavily upon imitation, serves well to dispel the notion that Palestrina was lacking in the mastery of polyphony compared to his contemporaries. The work offers no evidence whatsoever of Palestrina's so-called conservatism, but rather is highly complex and difficult. The work is fully scored throughout, and heavy demand is placed upon the singers both in regard to constancy in singing and the extremes of range which treat the three upper parts equally. This should be considered a work for SSSA, not SSAA. Rhythm, intervals and melodic flow are all treated with complexity and will present problems to all but the most advanced choirs; it is an exciting example of its style and period.

Unacc.

Palestrina, G. P. (ed. P. Boepple) Mercury MC 12

"Magnificat"
(in the Fourth Mode)

SSAA Med. Diff. 7 min.

This work is an excellent example of the Palestrina genius for contrapuntal writing. The twelve text sections are scored alternately between a solo voice singing the plainsong (Gregorian chant) and the choral sections of imitative counterpoint. The edition, like all the Mercury publications under Paul Boepple's editorship, is quite readable for amateur groups. The fourth mode, in which this work is scored, may present some tonality problems to amateur singers at first; however, no other major tonality problems exist. The system of un-measured bar lines (except between staves for visual help) seems to be a logical compromise to achieving textual fluidity. Two of the six choral sections are scored only for SSA, and the last section is more homophonic than the others, although counterpoint is still employed.

Unacc. a-f''

Peerson, Martin (ed. Peter Warlock) Ox 339

"Cuckoo"

SS | Easy | 1 min.

This is a simple madrigal-type work, for two equal voices, which is scored for vocal lines of a highly independent nature. Nevertheless the composition is not difficult. The echoing of the two vocal parts is charming and the number of sections are scored in duet style. Peerson became master of the choristers and organist at St. Paul's Cathedral and was a composer of instrumental and sacred choral music as well as secular works. The original accompaniment is for strings in three parts, but the piano accompaniment given is suitable for performance. The vocal lines are highly diatonic and offer no real rhythmic or harmonic problems. Dynamic variations are abundant throughout.

Accomp. c'-f''

<u>Peerson, Martin</u> (ed. Peter Warlock) Ox 339

"Come Pretty Wag"

SS | Easy | 1 min.

This work is very easy, yet very delightful, and in modified madrigal-style. The voice parts are highly independent, although they occasionally join for duet sections which remain simple, yet effective. The original accompaniment is for strings in three parts, but the piano accompaniment supplied is suitable. While the melodic and harmonic sections of this work are quite simple, the rhythmic syncopation may necessitate some special attention during first readings of the work.

Piano e'-e''

<u>Pergolesi, Giovanni</u> P 5363

"Stabat Mater"

SA (SA) | Med. | 46 min.

This work by Pergolesi is one of the most famous extended works for women's voices, and deservingly so. The duet and chorus sections contain some of the finest two-part writing (duet style) in the entire repertoire. In these sections can be found counterpoint, parallel movement, dissonances, suspensions and imitative writing, all skillfully treated. The solos are lyrical, rhythmic, expressive and sensitively constructed in every instance. In addition, the accompaniment, which is often independent material, is an important part of the entire structure. The work depends heavily upon this accompaniment for its overall effect. This selection is most effective in performance, especially so to the performers. It is certainly within the ability level of high school groups as well as those of the collegiate level.

String orchestra (or organ or piano) c'-g''

GS, Kalmus, Ox. R 45422

Peters, Flor De Ring, Antwerp

"Quatuor Motetta" (Op. 14)

SSA Diff. approx. 2 min. each

1. O Salutaris Hostia
2. Ave Maria
3. Vitam Petit a te
4. Tantum Ergo

These four motets are a welcome addition to sacred Latin literature (of short length) in the contemporary idiom. All except the fourth feature considerable independence of parts. However, each is characterized by a substantial amount of parallel movement, resulting in some degree of homophony and medieval flavor. There are a number of interesting points of dissonance throughout and the first three of the motets contain sections of brief imitative lines. The best of the four is number three ("Vitam"), if only because of its greater sense of unity and harmonic conception. The accompaniments, for the most part, support the vocal material.

Organ a-g''

Pfautsch, Lloyd Flammer 89204

"Fanfare for Christmas"

SSAA Med. 1 min.

This brief, jubilant fanfare is a welcome addition to the repertoire for women's voices. It is an excellent opening selection for a Christmas program. Practically all other existing fanfares for similar purposes are for mixed voices. The work must be performed with two trumpets and two trombones as originally scored. With this accompaniment, the work gains majestic excitement, as the voices alternate brief passages with the instruments in a semi-Gabrieli style. The vocal lines are quite rhythmic, as the composer employs brief elements of syncopation. The harmonies are not difficult, and those of the instruments are usually repeated from, or in sequence to, those of the vocal lines.

2 Trumpets and 2 trombones a-a''

Pinkham, Daniel ECS 2586

"If Ye Love Me"

SSA Med. 2 min.

This is a relatively easy composition by Pinkham, whose works are often beyond the performing level of amateur choirs. The work contains frequent shifts of meter, but if the text is carefully studied for normal accentuations, the meter shifts should present no major difficulties. The accompaniment is also simply scored and complements the choral setting of the text. The accompaniment often duplicates the choral harmonies, and in this way supports the vocal sections. There are three unison passages in the work which provide a refreshing contrast to the harmonic scoring. The choral progressions are not difficult, yet provide some modern sounds throughout the work.

Organ b-f#''

Pinkham, Daniel ECS 2572

"Three Lenten Poems of Richard Crashaw"

SSA Diff. 5 min.

I. On the Still Surviving Marks of Our Savior's Wounds

II. Upon the Body of Our Blessed Lord, Naked and Bloody

III. O Save Us Then

This work was commissioned by the Wheelock College (Boston) Alumnae Association and Glee Club. The work is difficult, mainly because of the intense dissonance throughout. The second composition is scored for unison chorus; however, the dissonances are still prevalent between the chorus line and the accompaniment. The work presents no rhythmic difficulties whatever, and although there are frequent shifts of meter, they are not difficult to negotiate, even for a true amateur choir. The first two selections of the group are rather placid and in a sostenuto style, the main emphasis being directed to melodic interest. The third selection is more dramatic in effect and provides a marked contrast to the first two pieces. The harmonic elements also receive more emphasis in this third selection, and the dissonances are more poignant.

Str. Quartet (or str. orch.) b-g''
and Handbells (or clesta or harp)
or keyboard accomp.

Poulenc, Francis

"Litanies"
a la Vierge Noire

SSA Med. 8-10 min.

1. The Good Little Girl
2. The Lost Dog
3. When Coming Home from School
4. The Little Sick Dog
5. The Hedgehog

This work by Poulenc is filled with a great deal of parallel voice movement, often based on chant-like melodies. Frequent changes of meter lend great interest and variety to the work, and a few syncopated phrase beginnings offer additional rhythmic variety. While the vocal parts are relatively reasonable throughout most of the work, there are some sections near the end which contain difficult intervals, especially in the second soprano part, and some of the harmonies are of a more dissonant nature than the preceding sections. The typical French idiomatic composition style is well represented in this work, and its effect is highly musical. If necessary, each selection could be performed separately.

Orchestra or organ g-a''

Scarlatti, Alessandro Ric NY 1894

"Stabat Mater"

SA (SA) Med. 35 min.

Though overshadowed by the better known Pergolesi work of the same title, this setting of the well-known "Stabat Mater" text by Scarlatti is deserving of more attention than has been accorded it in recent years. The form of the composition is very much like that of the Pergolesi work. It is comprised of a series of solos and choruses, with one duet included. The solo sections far outnumber the choruses; two of them (both for contralto) are actually recitatives, an obvious musical vehicle for a composer of predominantly operatic fame. The style of the "Stabat Mater" is essentially that of a series of solos and duets with basso continuo accompaniment. Scarlatti employs a large amount of chromaticism in this work, both in the vocal lines and in the accompaniment. From a harmonic standpoint, the work seems advanced for its time. While the chorus sections in this work are relatively easy, the solo sections are far more difficult.

Strings and piano (or organ) g-g'' (chorus parts)

Schubert, Franz Mercury MC 15

"Serenade"
"Ständchen" (Op. 135)

SSAA (A) Diff. 5-1/2 min.

This work was composed by Schubert at the request of his friend Anna Froehlich in 1827. It includes a very extensive and important alto solo, which, while not technically demanding, is the "heart" of the composition. In fact, this work might be categorized as an alto solo with chorus accompaniment. In addition to all of the vocal material, the work is also scored for full piano accompaniment throughout. Though the choral parts are not melodically difficult, Schubert has scored them in such a way that only the choir with good vocal control should attempt to perform this work. Many subtle and difficult dynamic shadings are included in these vocal lines and produce technical challenges which must be considered.

Piano g-b♭''

N. Trios 16

Schubert, Franz (ed. Max Spicker) GS 9110

"The Lord Is My Shepherd"
(Gott meine Zunersicht)
(Psalm 23)

SSAA Med. 8 min.

There seems to be considerable difficulty in finding good women's literature from the nineteenth century, but surely this work by Schubert contains many stylistic features common to that period. The work is in a homophonic style throughout, and features large amounts of chromatically moving harmonies which are characteristic of early Romantic music. The tempo indication by Schubert is slow, the accompaniment is scored in arpeggiated triplet figures, and numerous passages are carefully marked for crescendi and diminuendi; all of these features contribute to a typically Romantic setting of this famous Psalm text. A number of brief passages are set in duet style between the two upper or two lower parts, but the majority of the work is in full four-part harmony.

Piano or organ a^{b}-a^{b}''

N. Trios 67, O1-Dit 3196

Schumann, R. N 166

"The Steadfast Heavens"

(Op. 144 N. 3)

SSS Med. 2 min.

This work, the third in a group of three compositions in Schumann's Op. 114, appears to have a better text than the others. The work is scored in such a way that each voice takes up the original melody while a second, and then a third, harmony part is added to each successive presentation of the melodic material. The vocal parts are not difficult and the work benefits greatly from the fine piano accompaniment. Despite the seeming three verses, or three presentations of the same melodic material, the text is the same for all three. The work ends with a three-part treatment of the text which is effectively accompanied by the piano.

Piano a-g''

Schuman, William GS 8481

"Prelude for Women's Voices"

SSAA (S) Diff. 6 min.

This work, composed in 1939 when the composer was the conductor of the Sarah Lawrence College Chorus, is a stirring and very exciting composition. The text by Thomas Wolfe lends itself well to a choral setting of this type. While there are numerous phrases of chromatic voice leadings (all handled logically and thoughtfully by the composer), the work is still largely diatonic and much of it is homophonic, with no polyphony used. The lyric soprano solo is a most effective addition, beneath which the vocal parts are scored in supportive harmony. A good soloist with a fine sense of intonation and rhythmic security is essential to the desired free-flowing effect, although the solo itself is not difficult. Changes of meter signature and tempo are present, but pose no difficulties. Two unusual sections of the work are one in which the chorus whispers rhythmically beneath the soloist and another at the ending in which the altos sing 19 measures of pedal point "d" beneath the closing phrases of the soloist.

Piano g-g''

Schuman, William GS 8928

"Requiescat"

SSAA Diff. 2 min.

This work, composed in 1942 for the Sarah Lawrence College Chorus and later arranged for mixed voices, is a rather unusual and difficult number. The two-part counterpoint is quite misleading, for its visual simplicity is betrayed by rather difficult intervals and difficult dissonances which include augmented ninths, diminished fourths and minor seconds. The work is very effective, both in its contrapuntal vocal lines and its rich, full accompaniment. There is no text; the chorus is directed only to hum throughout. The work employs an alternating meter shift between 4/4 and 3/4 for the first six measures and then settles down to a 4/4 meter for the rest of its length. The accompaniment is abandoned near the end, with the final twelve measures sung mostly in two-part counterpoint. The final two chords are scored in four-part harmony.

Piano a^{b}-e''

Schütz, H. (ed. C. Buell Agey) Brodt WC 1

(Kleine geistliche Konzerte Bk. 1 No. 9)

"Blessed Is He Who Walks Not in the Paths of Godlessness"
(Wohl dem, der nicht wandelt im Rath der Gottlosen)

SA Med. 2-1/2 min.

This work is very similar in style to the other two-part compositions from Schütz' Kleine geistliche Konzerte collection. The manner of scoring the vocal material is that of presenting the melody one phrase at a time, with the second voice repeating the preceding phrase at a different pitch level. Occasionally, an entire phrase is presented prior to its repetition at another pitch, but often the repetition begins before the preceding presentation has been completed. This results in excellent two-part contrapuntal writing. The work is diatonic and employs no difficult harmonic or rhythmic elements. Schütz does include several changes of tempo and meter, which provide variety and contrasts within the work.

Organ a-g''

Schütz, H. (ed. P. Boepple) MP MC 17

"Great Is Our Lord"
(Der Herr ist Gross)

SS Med. 2-1/2 min.

This is one of several selections for equal voices which are typical of Schütz' style. The chief characteristic of this work is essentially that of imitative counterpoint, which often presents the two vocal lines in an alternating pattern of phrase presentation. The alternating pattern is occasionally abandoned, however, giving way to a duet style. The work is diatonic throughout, but many long melismas occur in each of the vocal lines, which accounts for the "medium" grade assignment listed in this annotation. This selection would be effective sung by solo voices, small chorus or a larger group, provided the sections of the large groups are balanced and capable of producing a light and fluid sound.

Organ, harpsichord or piano (BC) c'f''

Schütz, H. (ed. C. Buell Agey) Con 98-1558

"O Gracious Lord Our God"
(Sacred Concert Book I No. 6)

SS (2 equal) Med. 3 min.

This duet begins with a twelve-measure phrase by soprano I which is then repeated by soprano II. The first soprano part joins this repeated section and provides sections of both duet style and canonic imitation. Following three coda-like measures to the first section, the meter switches from duple to triple for sixteen measures of canonic writing, which serves as a second section to the composition. Following a brief return to the style of the opening section, the music then returns to triple meter for a longer section of canonic imitation which also employs some small amounts of seventeenth-century duet-style writing. The vocal parts are not particularly difficult; however, there are a few minor shifts of modality which may cause some pitch inaccuracies during early readings.

Organ c'-f''

Schütz, H. (ed. William Herrmann) Con 98-1414

"Sing O Ye Saints"
(Ihr Heiligen, Lobsinget dem Herren)

SS or SA (2 equal) Med. 3 min.

This is another duet from the Kleine geistliche Konzerte collection. Much of the two-part writing occurs as alternating phrase patterns between the two voices, often based upon imitative melodic patterns. The work is not difficult in either its harmonic or melodic elements, but the rhythm of many of the melismas is difficult to articulate with full sections of sopranos (or sopranos and altos). There are a number of modal "shifts" occurring in the melodic material which need careful attention, and these, combined with the long melismas and the rhythmic problems, make the work more of a challenge than appears from a simple perusal of the score.

Organ a-e''

Shaw, Martin Cur 71470

"Sylvia Sleeps"
(No. 3 of Four Pastorals)

SA Easy 1-1/2 min.

This is a simple setting in two parts, with arpeggiated piano accompaniment. The harmonic progressions are rather interesting, as the composer employs a modal-type shift between e minor (with its f# leading tone) and f major, with its b^b subdominant chord. Another interesting feature is the phrase structure, which is comprised of a five-measure phrase followed by a six-measure phrase. Following a two-measure piano interlude, this same pattern is repeated in a second verse. The work closes with an augmentation of the first two-measure pattern. The accompaniment, while quite simple, is very important to the effectiveness of this number.

Piano g-f''

Shaw, Martin GS 10041
(Curwen catalog)

"With a Voice of Singing"

SSA (divisi) Med. 2-1/2 min.

This is the well-known Anthem, originally scored for mixed voices, which the composer successfully rescored for women's voices. The work is highly spirited and energetic in its effect. Essentially, it is homophonic in style, although imitative entrances occur in several places, and the "pyramiding" effect of the "Alleluias" implies strong independence of vocal lines. Occasional phrases scored in unison lend excellent contrast to the otherwise fully-scored sections. The predominantly independent organ accompaniment, which is used to good effect, also provides interesting variety throughout the work.

Organ f#-g''

Smith, Dorothy Ox 582

"No Rose of Such Vertu"

SSAA (divisi) Diff. 3 min.

This popular text has been set again with success in this composition by Smith. Employing frequent modulations and meter changes, the work conveys an almost mystical effect to the listener. The first verse is scored in a modern homophonic style, sung by the three lower voices. The second verse is given over to a first soprano solo, while the three lower voices hum some unusual chordal progressions. The verse continues in an alternating pattern between the soprano voice and the lower three voices. The third verse returns to the pattern of the first, but with a first soprano descant line being added partway through. The final verse returns to the style of the first, being sung only by the three lower voices, beginning with the opening melody in a semi-cyclic form.

Unacc. g-ab''

Smith, Melville W 3W2722

"Lully, Lullay"

SSAA Med. -Diff. 2-1/2 min.

This is an unusually lovely and tender melody set with both contrapuntal (non-imitative) and chordal vocal support. Frequent meter changes, while adding to the difficulty of the work, nevertheless enhance the text accents considerably. The work contains some fairly unusual progressions of chords, but no difficult chords. The chords are not dissonant in any modern sense, yet the work has a distinctively modern sound. The anonymous text is effective and the composer treats the contrasting sections appropriately, ranging from lyrical flowing phrases to the more marcato type, to portray the sinister role of Herod. Following these contrasts, the work returns to the tender flow of the opening section.

Unacc. f-g''

Stanford, C. V. (ed. WGW) Ox 108

"Vitue"

SA | Easy | 3 min.

This is an exceptionally fine two-part work, completely through-composed. The accompaniment is quite independent. The work is not difficult, yet the effect is that of some degree of complexity. The two voice parts are often independent, yet combine in many sections in duet style. The text by G. Herbert is artistic, despite the misleading title. The accompaniment, which is very effective, often employs a two-note descending "motive" which the voice parts also occasionally take up. This is a selection which is surely worthy of the attention of conductors whose choirs cannot handle more complex and difficult writing. The effect is that of high quality and workmanship, but the work is without the technical demands so often associated with such selections.

Piano d'-g"

Thompson, Randall ECS 2539

"Come In"
(from Frostiana)

SSA (divisi) | Med. | 4-1/2 min.

Two of the seven selections of the Frostiana collection are for women's voices, the rest being for either male or mixed voices. "Come In", with text by Robert Frost, is the first of the women's numbers. This work is totally homophonic in style, yet contains many challenging demands upon a chorus to produce the subtleties and shadings of contrasting nuances and dynamic variations. One of the most impressive elements of the composition is the piano accompaniment, which has the responsibility of setting the mood for the entire performance. Only the most musically sensitive of accompanists should be entrusted to the role. The harmonies of the vocal lines are not difficult, but the chordal changes are effectively scored in a variation between simple consonance and simple dissonance.

Piano g-g"

Thompson, Randall ECS 1985

"Now I Lay Me Down to Sleep"

SSA | Easy | 1-1/2 min.

This is a simple but effective contrapuntal setting of the familiar child's prayer. It is based on imitative counterpoint which is uncomplicated in modal harmony or poly-textual effects. It would serve as an excellent introduction to contrapuntal style for an amateur chorus with little or no previous experience in singing polyphonic music. It is musically worthwhile as well. There are no difficult intervals or harmonic effects, yet independence of vocal lines is stressed by means of imitative counterpoint.

Unacc. g-g''

Thompson, Randall ECS 492

"Pueri Hebraeorium"

SSAA-SSAA (Antiphonal) Med. 2-1/2 min.

There are few original works for women's voices in antiphonal style. This one is very effective in performance, especially when the two choirs are placed at opposite sides of the stage or church. This is a "festival-type" selection in that many of the passages are fully scored for eight parts, with the voices spread over the full practical compass of the choirs' tessitura. Brief echo-like passages produce a joyful interplay between choruses and the dynamic contrasts add to the effectiveness of this interplay. Several shifts between duple and triple meter add excitement to the work, as does the occasional shift of tonality. The work contains some rhythmic complexities and some of the snycopations used will present some problems of ensemble in early readings.

Unacc. g-a''

Thompson, Randall ECS 2684

"The Lord Is My Shepherd"

SSAA Easy-Med. 9 min.

This is Randall Thompson's most recent work for women's voices. The style is often that which has identified Thompson's music for years; however, occasionally a chord progression or an accompaniment feature is new. The choral sections are simply set, with long interludes by the accompaniment between sections of the text. The work contains several modulations, but each is presented with adequate preparation in the accompaniment before the vocal entrances. Only one change of meter is introduced, and that is from 12/8 to 4/4, using the same four pulses per measure.

This selection exhibits considerable dynamic contrasts, but few tempo changes other than rallentandos and normal returns to a tempo.

Piano, organ or harp

f#-a''

Vaughn-Williams, Ralph

Cur 71571

"It Was a Lover and His Lass"

SS

Diff.

2 min.

This text by Shakespeare has had many choral settings, but none as fresh and interesting as this one by the deceased "dean" of English contemporary music. While the setting is for only two equal voices, it is nevertheless a fine work. Its difficulty lies in the shifting of vocal parts between major and minor and also in a modal shift within the melodic and harmonic passages caused by the use of d natural in both E Major and E minor. The work also contains an occasional change of meter from 2/2 to 3/2, but this is not difficult. The accompaniment is both interesting and varied in style and lends considerable variety to the work. While this may be a difficult selection to learn, it is well worth the effort.

Piano

b-f#''

Vaughn-Williams, Ralph

Ox

"Lullaby"
(from the Cantata This Day)

SSA

Med.

3 min.

As in many of Vaughn-Williams' selections, this work has a folk idiom "ring" to the melodic and rhythmic style. It is a hauntingly lovely melody, most often set in two-part harmony with a descant-like part added. The "lullaby" text is interspersed frequently between lines of Ballet's somewhat familiar text. A few relatively easy changes of time signature are artfully employed for the sake of the text, and the entire selection is set in a minor key, with a modulation to the subdominant key, and a return to the tonic. The accompaniment is simply scored, doubling the vocal lines and adding additional harmonic and melodic elements.

Piano

g-f''

Vaughn-Williams, Ralph

Ox 46-200

"Magnificat"

SSAA (A)

Med.

12 min.

The choral parts of this work are not at all difficult, even though modern sonorities are used occasionally. The alto solo, which comprises more than half of the vocal portions, is quite difficult and demands a very mature and sensitive soloist. If orchestral parts (available from the publisher) are not used, a skillful accompanist and flutist are needed to perform this work. A large amount of the choral sections is scored for unison chorus and there are no difficult passages scored for chorus. A number of key changes occur throughout the selection, but none involve the chorus. In general the work is rather slow. While there are some dynamic contrasts indicated in the score, the tempos remain slow throughout.

Orch. (or fl. and piano) b-g'' (chorus)

Verdi, G. P 4256c

"Laudi alla Vergine Maria"
(Hymn to the Virgin)

SSAA Med. 5-1/2 min.

This selection is listed as number three in Verdi's "Four Sacred Pieces". It is his only known work for female choir. It is set in a solemn homophonic style, although brief sections of independent part writing are included. There are no meter or tempo changes indicated, and the harmonies are not difficult to sing. Some demands are made upon the soprano range, and there are long sostenuto phrases in all of the vocal parts. There are numerous changes of dynamic markings indicated throughout, although the majority of the work is placid and on a soft dynamic level.

Unacc. Ric 11457, AJB f#-a''

Vullieinoz, Marguerite L. Galaxy 999

"The Storke"

SSA Easy 3 min.

This is a skillful setting of a lovely melody; the text tells of the visit of the stork to the manger in Bethlehem. The work begins with unison sopranos for the first verse. The second soprano joins in on the second verse, and the alto part is added to the third verse. The design is strophic. The accompaniment is quite nice and varies considerably in the third verse. None of the vocal parts are difficult and the voice leadings are carefully treated to insure ease of performance and beauty of execution.

Piano or organ a^b-f''

Weelkes, Thomas Kalmus 233

"A Country Paire"

SSA Diff. 2-1/2 min.

This is a very difficult three-voice madrigal which demands strict adherence to the rhythmic syncopations. There is considerable independence of vocal parts, although the top two soprano parts are often treated in duet style. Imitation is characteristic of the vocal treatment, as is the use of suspensions, syncopations, and occasional harmonic shifts from major to minor. The two soprano parts are treated equally with regard to range, as the second soprano involves the same high register as the first. The alto part also presents range problems, as the alto line descends to a low "f" in several places.

Unacc. f-g''

Weelkes, Thomas (ed. EHF) SB 1802

"Late in My Rash Accounting"

SSA Med. 3 min.

This madrigal-style composition by Weelkes is exceptionally well constructed. The tempo is not too fast, and the "fa-la" refrain to each verse is highly sequential between the two soprano parts and the alto part. Melodically and harmonically, it demands complete independence among the parts, although the two soprano parts are treated in duet style almost completely throughout. A change of meter from 4/4 to 3/4 occurs halfway through the second half, which invests the work with some variety.

Unacc. f-g''

Weelkes, Thomas (ed. EHF) SB 1797

"The Gods Have Heard My Vows"

SSA Med. 2 min.

This is a fairly simple example of sixteenth-century madrigal-type composition, although this work might more properly be classified as an "air". The work contains an interesting combination of homophonic style combined with some independence of vocal parts. There are three verses contained in this selection, all set to the same melodic and harmonic materials, each with a short "fa-la" ending. There are no unusually difficult harmonic or melodic sections, as the work is essentially diatonic, especially in the melodic lines of the three voice parts. The work does contain an unmarked shift of meter for a brief two measures.

Unacc. g-g''

Weelkes, Thomas (ed. EHF) SB 1798

"Though My Carriage Be But Careless"

SSA Med. 1-1/2 min.

This is another air from the "Collection of Airs and Fantastic Spirits" by Weelkes catalogued under Vol. 13. The text makes it particularly well suited to women's voices. The work contains sufficient chromatic alterations in the lower parts to cause it to be a little difficult. The first half of the work is largely homophonic in style; the second half involves independence of vocal parts. Near the end of the work there is a fairly long pedal point in the first soprano part, which is somewhat unusual for a composition of this style period.

Unacc. a-e''

Wilbye, John SB M 6/2

"Away! Thou Shalt Not Love Me!"

SSA Med. 2 min.

This is a fine madrigal by the important English composer Wilbye. It is highly imitative in style, with considerable independence of vocal lines. Due to the rather brisk tempo and the almost constant points of imitation, the use of modern bar lines in this edition results in a fair degree of complex rhythms throughout the work. This produces a stirring melodic and rhythmic effect throughout the madrigal. The chief melodic figure employed is that of a descending scale pattern, first in a pattern of eighth notes and then in a dotted rhythm pattern in the second half of the work. This is a very exciting number to perform, and the counterpoint provides great interest.

Unacc. g-g''

Wilbye, John (ed. EHF) SB 1716

"Come Shepherd Swains"

SSA Med. 2-1/2 min.

This work is an interesting mixture of homophonic

and contrapuntal style. While there are numerous sections of vocal independence among the three vocal parts, many phrases have the two soprano parts in duet style, with an independent alto line. Other phrase sections are highly homophonic in the treatment of all three parts. Imitation is an important composition element, although in this selection it results in no rhythmic problems of any consequence. The harmony is predominantly diatonic, and the work presents no real performance difficulties, other than demands on extended ranges both high and low.

Unacc. f#-a''

Willan, Healey BM 1808

"Oh! Queen of Heaven"
(Regina Coeli Letare)

SSAA Med. 3 min.

This is a fine contemporary setting of the sixteenth-century text. While the vocal parts appear difficult, great care in the handling of voice leadings and the frequent treatment of two parts as a unit (altos against sopranos) actually result in a lessening of the apparent problems, so that the work is not too complex or difficult. There are a few measures in which the vocal lines are independent; however, for the most part the work moves in extensive parallel design, both rhythmically and melodically. An occasional shift of time signature presents no problems, and the text obviously benefits from the resulting correct placing of accents. This is a work which has been seriously neglected for no good reason. The work is fully scored throughout, with the full chorus singing most of the time.

Unacc. g^b-a^b''

Williams, Catherine GS 8446

"At Chrystemesse-Tyde"

SSAA Diff. 2 min.

This is quite a different and unusual Christmas selection, with a fine text by Willis Boyd Allen ("Two Sorrie Thyngs There Be"). The musical setting is equally effective, although somewhat difficult in sections. The voice leading is well conceived, as the composer, anticipating vocal difficulties of the average choir, has taken care to score the vocal parts smoothly and logically. In this regard, there are many sections in which the two soprano parts are treated as a unit and are contrasted with the unit of two alto parts.

This helps to make the work easier to perform, as well as more structurally unified. The lack of accompaniment puts more responsibility on the singers, but the work certainly is in no need of accompaniment either for harmonic or rhythmic support, or as a means of providing variety.

Unacc. f#-a''

Youll, Henry (ed. EHF) SB 2475-20

"Come, Merry Lads, Let Us Away"

SSA Med. 1-1/2 min.

This is a merry canzonet of the English madrigal school (early seventeenth century) by the little known composer, Henry Youll. The work is both homophonic and contrapuntal, containing a happy mixture of both styles. The work is light and gay, and the voice parts are relatively simple and uncomplex. Each vocal line is treated in a diatonic fashion, and the resulting harmony offers no unusual key or modal changes. Even the rhythm, which employs rhythmic and harmonic suspension at cadence points, presents no problem in execution. The work has a considerable degree of variety built into it, and the second half of the composition employs considerable independence of vocal parts.

Unacc. g-d''

Youll, Henry (ed EHF) SB 2475-19

"In the Merry Month of May"

SSA Med. 2 min.

This is a delightful, fast moving canzonet, complete with a "fa-la" section which is sheer delight to sing. Considerable independence of voice parts is evident throughout the work, but the vocal lines are so logically and melodically conceived that little or no performance problems are apparent. Imitation is predominant, and the "echoing" effect of the "fa-la's" between the voices is both fresh and exciting. Sequential patterns in the points of imitation are employed as a composition technique, but they are easy to sing. Neither harmony, melody nor rhythm is a problem anywhere within this work and, except for an occasional low "g" in the alto part, the vocal range is quite conservative.

Unacc. g-e''

V. Recommended Arrangements

Aichinger, Gregor — Ric NY 1848

"Regina Coeli"
(Not the same composition as W 2900)

SSA
(Unacc.) — Ruggero Veni', arr.

Arcadelt, Jacob — ECS 1540

"Hear Thou My Prayer, O Lord"
("Ave Maria")

SSAA
(Unacc.) — Katherine K. Davis, arr.

Bach, J. S. — ECS 1051

"O Jesu So Sweet"
(O Jesulein süss)

SSAA
(Unacc.) — Katherine K. Davis, arr.

Barthelson, Joyce (Arr.) — LG 767

"Ding Dong, Merrily on High"

SSA
(Piano) — Joyce Barthelson, arr.

Bartholomew, M. (Arr.) — GS 9311

"Riddle Song"
("I Gave My Love a Cherry")

SSAA
(Unacc.) — M. Bartholomew, arr.

Bennet, John (Arr.) — Gray 512

"All Creatures Now Are Merry Minded"

SSA
(Unacc.) — John Bennet, arr.

Best, Jack (Arr.) — Shawnee Press B-158

"Three Highland Airs"

I Ae Fond Kiss
II Bonnie George Campbell
III Rest My Ain Bairnie

SSA
(Piano) — Jack Best, arr.

Bortniansky, D. — Gray 1000

"Cherubic Song"

SSA
(Unacc.)

Albert Ham, arr.

Brahms, J.

LG 51181

1. Down Low in the Valley
2. The Still of Night

SSA
(Unacc.)

Ivan Trusler, arr.

Brahms, J.

ECS 189

"Four Love Songs"

1. Was Once a Pretty, Tiny Birdie (Op. 52 N. 6)
2. In Wood Embowered, 'neath Azure Skies (Op. 52 N. 9)
3. No There Is No Bearing with These Spiteful Neighbors (Op. 52 N. 11)
4. Secret Nook in Shady Spot (Op. 65 N. 8)

SSA
(4-hand Piano)

H. Clough-Leighter, arr.

Brahms, J.

ESV 855

"Magdalena"

SSAA
(Unacc.)

E. Harold Geer, arr.

Brahms, J.

ESV 896

"Praise of Mary"
(Marias Lob)

SSAA
(Unacc.)

E. Harold Geer, arr.

Brahms, J.

ESV 897

"Mary's Pilgrimage"
(Marias Wallfahrt)

SSAA
(Unacc.)

E. Harold Geer, arr.

Brahms, J.

ESV 886

"The Hunter"
(Der Jäger)

SSAA
(Unacc.)

E. Harold Greer, arr.

Brahms, J.

ECS 2505

"The Trysting Place" (Op. 31 N. 3)

(Der Gang Zum Liebehen)

SSA (Piano) — Victoria Glaser, arr.

<u>Brahms, J.</u> — ECS 879

"Three Chorals from Motets Op. 29 N. 1 and Op. 74"

1. To Us Salvation Now Is Come
2. In Peace and Joy I Now Depart
3. O Saviour, Open Heaven Wide

SSAA (Unacc.) — E. Harold Geer, arr.

<u>Brasart, Johannes</u> — MP DCS 28

"O Flos Flagrans"
(A Song to the Blessed Virgin Mary)
(Note: correct title should be "O Flos Fragrans")

SSA (Unacc.) — Paul Boepple, ed.

<u>Burleigh, H. T.</u> (Arr.) — Ric NY 693

"Were You There?"

SSA (Unacc.) — H. T. Burleigh, arr.

<u>Burt, Alfred</u> — Shawnee Press B-161

"The Alfred Burt Carols"
(Set I)

1. Caroling, Caroling
2. All On a Christmas Morning
3. We'll Dress the House
4. Ah, Bleak and Chill the Wintry Wind

SSA (Unacc.) — Hawley Ades, transcr.

<u>Burt, Alfred</u> — Shawnee Press B-160

"The Alfred Burt Carols"
(Set II)

1. Oh Hearken Ye
2. Some Children See Him
3. Jesu Parvule
4. Bright, Bright the Holly Berries
5. The Star Carol

SSA (Unacc.) — Hawley Ades, transcr.

<u>Byrd, Wm.</u> — SB 4873

"Cradle Song"

SSA Edmund Horace Fellowes, arr.
(Piano)

Byrd, Wm. ECS 815

"Sacerdotes Domini"

SSAA G. Wallace Woodworth, arr.
(Unacc.)

Carissimi, G. BM 11061

"O Felix Anima"

SSA C. A. Garabedian, adapt.
(Unacc.)

Clarke, Douglas (Arr.) BM 1838

"I Saw Three Ships Come Sailing In"

SSAA Douglas Clarke, arr.
(Unacc.)

Collins, Leo (Arr.) Row 6118

"Susanni"
(German Folk Song)

SSA Leo Collins, arr.
(Unacc.)

Collins, Leo (Arr.) Row 6117

"Mary's Lullaby"

SSA Leo Collins, arr.
(Unacc.)

Collins, Leo (Arr.) Row R6111

"The Rich Old Miser"

SSA Leo Collins, arr.
(Piano)

Cope, Cecil (Arr.) Bo Ha 1895

"Ten Christmas Carols"

(Intro.) Gloria in Excelsis Deo!
1. I Sing of a Maiden
2. What Is this Odour Round Us Flowing?
3. Wassail Song
4. Joseph, Joseph
5. A Babe Lies in the cradle
6. Quem Pastores
(Shepherds Loud Their Praises Singing)

7. In Dulci Jubilo
   (Good Christian Men Rejoice)
8. The Holly and the Ivy
9. The Angel Sang
10. A Little Child There Is y-Born

SSA (Unacc.) — Cecil Cope, arr.

Copland, Aaron (adapted) — Bo Ha 5025

"Ching-A-Ring-Chaw"
(Minstrel Song)

SSAA (Piano) — Irving Fine, arr.

Copland, Aaron (adapted) — Bo Ha 1903

"Simple Gifts"
(Shaker Song)

SA (Piano) — Irving Fine, arr.

Croce, Giovanni — 01-Dit 14, 209

"In Monte Oliveti"
("Upon the Mount of Olives")

SSA (Unacc.) — Louis Victor Saar, arr.

Crueger, Johann — Con 18

"Jesu, Priceless Treasure"

SSA (Unacc.) — H. J. Markworth, setting & arr.

Cui, Cesar — ECS 1081

"Radiant Stars, Above the Mountains Flowing"

SSAA (Piano) — Katherine K. Davis, arr.

d'Astorga, Emmanuel — ECS 1983

"Christe, quum sit jam exire"
("Christ, Now At Thy Passion" from Stabat Mater)

SSA (Organ) — Victoria Glaser, arr.

Davison, Archibald T. (Arr.) — ECS 1513

"Turn Ye to Me"

SSA (Piano) — Archibald T. Davison, arr.

Davis, Katherine K. (Arr.) Summy B-140

"I Gave My Love a Pretty Little Ring"

SSA Katherine K. Davis, arr.
(Piano)

Davis, Katherine K. (Arr.) ECS 1058

"Tween the Mount and Deep, Deep Vale"

SSA Katherine K. Davis, arr.
(Piano)

Debussy, Claude GS 5992

"The Rain Falls on My Heart"
("Il Pleure dans Mon Coeur")

SSAA (divisi) Jeanne Boyd, arr.
(Piano)

Des Préz, Josquin ECS 816

"Ave Verum"

SSA G. Wallace Woodworth, arr.
(Unacc.)

Dickinson, Clarence (Arr.) Gray 259

"Angels O'er the Fields"

SSAA
(Organ *ad lib.*) Clarence Dickinson, arr.

Dowland, John ECS 1085

"Come Again! Sweet Love Doth Now Invite"

SSAA Katherine K. Davis, arr.
(Unacc.)

Dowland, John JF 7377

"Say, Love, If Ever Thou Didst Find"

SSA Gwynn S. Bement, arr.
(Unacc.)

Erb, James (Arr.) LG 51036

"Medieval Triptych"

I Gregorian Chant
II Conductus (early 13th Century)
III Motet (late 13th Century)

SSA James Erb, arr.
(Percussion)

Ericksen, Frederick (Arr.) Gray 1261

"Deck the Halls"

SSA Frederick Ericksen, arr.
(Unacc.)

Frackenpohl, Arthur (Arr.) Mills 683

"The Bird's Song"

SSA Arthur Frackenpohl, arr.
(Piano)

Gasparini, Quirino GS 8154

"Adoramus Te"

SSAA Katherine K. Davis, arr.
(Unacc.)

Geer, E. Harold (Arr.) ECS 822

"Ding Dong! Merrily on High"

SSAA E. Harold Geer, arr.
(Unacc.)

Geer, E. Harold (Arr.) ECS 1919

"Christ the Lord Hath Risen"

SSA E. Harold Geer, arr.
(Unacc.)

Geer, E. Harold (Arr.) ESV 898

"Noel Nouvelet"
(Sing a New Noel)

SSAA (S) E. Harold Geer, arr.
(Unacc.)

Gevaert, Francois W 3W 2858

"Joyous Christmas Song"
(Chanson Joyeuse de Noel)

SSAA Max T. Krone, arr.
(Unacc.)

Gibbons, Orlando ECS 1932

"O Lord, Increase My Faith"

SSAA Arthur S. Talmadge, arr.
(Unacc.)

Gibbons, Orlando SB 251

"The Silver Swan"

SSA Edmund Horace Fellowes, adapt.

(Unacc.)

Glaser, Victoria (Arr.) ECS 1959

"The Twelve Days of Christmas"

SSAA (S) Victoria Glaser, arr.
(Piano)

Handl, Jacob GS 8441

"Pueri Concinite"
("Children Come")

SSAA E. Harold Geer, ed.
(Unacc.)

Hassler, Hans L. ECS 1887

"Cantate Domino"
(O Sing unto The Lord)

SSAA Gwynn S. Bement, arr.
(Unacc.)

Hassler, Hans L. ECS 1918

"Crucifixus Etiam pro Nobis"
(from the Credo Mass I)

SA Arthur S. Talmadge, ed. & arr.
(Unacc.)

Holst, Imogen (Arr.) Ox 2470

"Six Traditional Carols"

1. The Holly and the Ivy
2. Joys Seven
3. A Virgin Most Pure
4. I Saw Three Ships
5. Bedfordshire Mayday Carol
6. Matthew, Mark and Luke and John

SSA Imogen Holst, arr.
(Unacc.)

Isaac, Heinrich ECS 1923

"My Only Joy in All the World"

SSAA Victoria Glaser, arr.
(Unacc.)

Jacob, Gordon (Arr.) Ox 558

"Brother James' Air"

SSA Gordon Jacob, arr.
(Piano)

Jonequin, Clement ECS 1987

"Ce Moys de May"
(This Month of May)

SSA
(Piano)
Alfred Finch, arr.

Jungst, Hugo (Arr.) Gray

"While Shepherds Watched Their Sheep"

SSAA
(Unacc.)
Hugo Jungst, arr.

Kent, Richard (Arr.) LG 51216

"Fare Thee Well, O Honey"

SSA
(Unacc.)
Richard Kent, arr.

Kodaly, Z. (Arr.) Ox 503

"See the Gipsy"

SSAA
(Unacc.)
Z. Kodaly, arr.

Kodaly, Z. (Arr.) Ox 502

"The Straw Guy"

SSAA
(Unacc.)
Z. Kodaly, arr.

Kubik, Gail Southern

"Little Bird, Little Bird"

SSSSAAAA
(Piano)
John Klein, arr.

Kubik, Gail (Arr.) GS 9995

"Oh Dear! What Can the Matter Be?"

SSA (divisi)
(Unacc.)
Gail Kubik, arr.

Lasso, Orlando di ECS 1811

"Echo Song"

SSA-SSA
(Unacc.)
Elizabeth Marting, arr.

Lasso, Orlando di 01-Dit 332-13101

"Matona, Lovely Maiden"

SSA
Louis Victor Saar, arr.

(Unacc.)

Lathrop, Roy (Arr.) Pro-Art 1020

"Whistle and I'll Come to You"
(Scotch Tune)

SSA Roy Lathrop, arr.
(Piano)

Leontovich, M. CF CM 5276

"Carol of the Bells"

SSA Peter Wilhousky, arr.
(Unacc.)

Lotti, Antonio ECS 1949

"Agnus Dei"
(Lamb of God)
(from Mass VII)

SSAA Arthur S. Talmadge, arr.
(Unacc.)

Lotti, Antonio ECS 1904

"Kyrie"
(from Mass VII)

SSAA Arthur S. Talmadge, arr.
(Unacc.)

Lotti, Antonio Remick 3-G 1541

"Regina Coeli"
(Queen of the Heavens)

SSAA
(Unacc.) Don Malin, arr.

Lotti, Antonio ECS 1509

"Vere Languores Nostros"
(Surely He Hath Borne Our Grief)

SSA G. Wallace Woodworth, arr.
(Unacc.)

Lvovsky, S. V. HWG 1536

"Hospodi Pomilui"

SSAA Boris Levenson, transcr.
(Unacc.)

Menegali, Martin Joseph BM 11421

"Ave Regina"

SSA (Unacc.) C. A. Garabedian, adapt.

Mendelssohn, F. GS 4371

"How Lovely Are the Messengers"
(from St. Paul)

SSA (Piano) Max Spicker, arr.

Morales, Cristobal de GS 11077

"O Magnum Mysterium"

SSAA (Unacc.) Robert Goudale, ed.

Morley, Thomas GS 8156

"April Is in My Mistress' Face"

SSAA (Unacc.) Katherine K. Davis, arr.

Morley, Thomas JF 7415

"Come Lovers, Follow Me"

SSA (Unacc.) Gwynn S. Bement, arr.

Morley, Thomas Hall & McCr. 2068

"Fire, Fire My Heart"

SSAA (Unacc.) Kenneth Runkel, arr.

Morley, Thomas 01-Dit 13568

"It Was a Lover And His Lass"

SSAA (Unacc.) Arthur Fagge, arr.

Morley, Thomas JF 7593

"I Will No More"
(from "Madrigalls to Foure Voyces")

SSAA (Unacc.) Gwynn S. Bement, arr.

Morley, Thomas N 483

"My Bonny Lass She Smileth"

SSAA (Unacc.) John West, arr.

Morley, Thomas ECS 825

"Now Is the Month of Maying"

SSAA G. Wallace Woodworth, arr.
(Unacc.)

Morley, Thomas N 479

"What Saith My Dainty Darling"

SSAA John West, arr.
(Unacc.)

Mueller, Carl F. (Arr.) GS 8159

"Blow, Winds, O Softly Blow"

SSA Carl F. Mueller, arr.
(Piano)

Niles, J. J. (Arr.) GS 8305

"I Wonder As I Wander"

SSAA (S) J. J. Niles, arr.
(Unacc.)

Niles, J. J. (Arr.) GS 9479

"Never Was a Child So Lovely"

SSAA J. J. Niles & Amand Parsons, arr.
(Unacc.)

Niles, John Jacob & GS 11206
Sheppard, J. Stanley (Arrs.)

"The Lass from the Low Countree"

SSAA John Jacob Niles &
(Piano) J. Stanley Sheppard, arrs.

Nin, Joaquin (Transcr.) AMP

"And the Angel Woke the Shepherds"
(No. 2 of Four Spanish Folk Songs)

SSAA
(Piano) Joaquin Nin, transcr.

Palestrina, G. P. ECS 1962

"Ascendit Deus"

SSAA Kenneth Runkel, arr.
(Unacc.)

Palestrina, G. P. JF 7302

"Benedictus"
(from Missa Brevis)

SSA Gwynn S. Bement, ed.
(Unacc.)

Palestrina, G. P. (et. al.) ESV 869

"Four Responses"

SSAA	1.	Gloria Patri	(Palestrina)
SSA	2.	Jesu Salvator Mundi	(Menegali)
SSA	3.	Non, Nobis, Domine	(Byrd)
SSAA	4.	Christus Factus Est	(Handl, J.)

(Unacc.) E. Harold Geer, arr. & ed.

Palestrina, G. P. JF 7422

"My Heart It Seemed Was Dying"
(Mori Quasi il mio core)

SSAA Gwynn S. Bement, arr.
(Unacc.)

Palestrina, G. P. ECS 1812

"O Bone Jesu"

SSAA H. Clough-Leighter, arr.
(Unacc.)

Parrish, Carl (setting) W 2W 8236

"Oh Rise Shine!"

SSA Carl Parrish, setting
(Unacc.)

Peerson, M. Galaxy 1082

"Upon My Lap My Soveraigne Sits"

SSAA Katherine K. Davis, arr.
(Unacc.)

Praetorius, Michael CF CM 411

"In Dulci Jubilo"

SA E. Harold Geer, transcr.
(Unacc.)

Praetorius, Michael ECS 1993

"In Natili Domini"
(At the Sweet Birth of Our Lord)

SSA Victoria Glaser, arr.
(Unacc.)

Purcell, H. ECS 487

"Sound The Trumpet"
("Welcome Song")

SA Alfred Moffat, arr.
(Piano)

Riegger, Wallingford (Arr.) Flammer 86048

"Beautiful Saviour"
(Crusader's Hymn)

SA (S) Wallingford Riegger, arr.
(Piano or organ)

Roselli, F. 01-Dit 14, 206

"Adoramus Te"

SSA
(Unacc.) Louis Victor Saar, arr.

Ryder, Wm. (Arr.) Ric NY 728

"Drink to Me Only"

SSAA Wm. Ryder, arr.
(Unacc.)

Schein, John H. Row 498

"Three Sacred Concerts for the Christmas Season"

I Now Come, the Heathen's Saviour
II All Praise Be Thine, Lord Jesus Christ
III From Heaven on High, I Come to You

SSA Edward Low & Daniel Pinkham, editors
(Organ)

Schubert, Franz LG 789

"The Echo"

SSA Wendell J. Rider, arr.
(Piano)

Schuman, Wm. (Arr.) GS 8948

"Holiday Song"

SSA Wendell J. Rider, arr.
(Piano)

Schuman, Wm. (Arr.) GS 9212

"The Orchestra Song"

6 parts Wm. Schuman, arr.
(any comb. of voices)
(Unacc.)

Schütz, H. GS 8981

"Veni, Rogo, in Cor Meum"

(Come I Pray Thee, Dwell Within Me)

SSAA E. Harold Geer, arr.
(Unacc.)

Spicker, Max (Arr.) GS 439

"While by My Sheep"
("Christmas Hymn")

SSAA Max Spicker, arr.
(Unacc.)

Stellhorn, A. W. (Arr.) Con 5

"Let Us All with Gladsome Voice"

SSAA A. W. Stellhorn, arr.
(Unacc.)

Sweelinck, Jan Pieters BM 2361

"Or Sus, Serviteurs du Seigneur"
(Arise, All Ye Servants of the Lord)
Psalm CXXXIV

SSAA Margaret Macdonald, arr.
(Unacc.)

Tallis, Thomas C F CM 402

"Nunc Dimittis"
(from Evening Service in Dorian Mode)

SSAA (or double choir) Arthur E. Egerton, arr.
(Unacc.)

Terri, Salli (Arr.) LG 666

"Away in a Manger"

SSA Salli Terri, arr.
(Opt. harp or piano)

Thiman, Eric H. (Arr.) Gray 2402

"O Brother Man"

SA (divisi) Eric H. Thiman, arr.
(Piano)

Thompson, Virgil (Arr.) Gray 2294

"My Shepherd Will Supply My Need"

SSAA Virgil Thompson, arr.
(Unacc.)

Tschesnokoff, Paul Bourne WE 7

"Salvation Is Created!"

SSA
(Unacc.)
Walter Ehret, arr.

Treharne, Bryceson (Setting) BM 1901

"Child in the Manger"

SSA
(Piano)
Bryceson Treharne, setting

Treharne, Bryceson (Setting) BM 1519

"Star Lullaby"

SA
(Piano)
Bryceson Treharne, setting

Treharne, Bryceson (Setting) BM 1527

"The Elfin Horn"

SSA
(Piano)
Bryceson Treharne, setting

Vaughn-Williams (Arr.) Ox

"Folk Songs of the Four Seasons"
(Cantata)

SSA
(Orch. or piano)
Vaughn-Williams, arr.

Vecchi, Orazio LG 741

"Sing Me a Song"
(Fa una Canzone)

SSAA
(Unacc.)
Jerry Weseley Harris, arr.

Vene', Ruggero (Arr.) AMP

Six French Folk Songs

1. Au Clair de la Lune (AMP 96)
2. Si le Roy M'avait Donne' (" 97)
3. Pavanne (" 98)
4. Les Trois Princesses (" 99)
5. En Passant par la Lorraine (" 100)
6. Jardin d'Amour (" 101)

SSA
(Piano)
Ruggero Vene', arr.

Vittoria, T. L. da JF 5050

"Ave Maria"

SSAA
(Unacc.)
D. Taylor, arr.

Vittoria, T. L. da — 01-Dit 13, 381

"Duo Seraphim"
("Lo, Two Seraphim")

SSAA — Kurt Schindler, ed.
(Unacc.)

Vittoria, T. L. da — ECS 1941

"Gaudent in Caelis"

SSAA — Arthur S. Talmadge, arr.
(Unacc.)

Vittoria, T. L. da — ECS 830

"Jesu, Dulcis Memoria"
(Jesus, the Very Thought of Thee)

SSAA — G. Wallace Woodworth, arr.
(Unacc.)

Vittoria, T. L. da — ECS 1922

"O Magnum Mysterium"

SSAA — Victoria Glaser, arr.
(Unacc.)

Vittoria, L. T. da — ESV 871

"O Vos Omnes"
(O Ye People)

SSAA — E. Harold Geer, ed.
(Unacc.)

Vittoria, T. L. da — ECS 1507

"Tanquam Agnus"

SSA — Archibald T. Davison, ed.
(Unacc.)

Vulpius, Melchoir — Gray 148

"An Easter Hallelujah"

SSAA-SSAA — E. Harold Geer, arr.
double chorus
(Unacc.)

Weelkes, T. — SB 252

"Sing We at Pleasure"

SSA — Edmund Horace Fellowes, adapt.
(Unacc.)

Weelkes, T. — 01-Dit 15099

"Welcome Sweet Pleasure"

SSA — Gwynn S. Bement, arr.
(Unacc.)

West, John (Arr.) — N 222

"The Bonnie Banks of Loch Lomond"

SA — John West, arr.
(Piano)

Weston, Philip (Arr.) — Elkan

"Greensleeves"

SSAA — Philip Weston, arr.
(Piano)

Wilbye, John — ECS 1076

"Adieu, Sweet Amarillas"

SSAA — Katherine K. Davis, arr.
(Unacc.)

Williams, John Gerrard (Arr.) — Cur 71563

"Early One Morning"

SA — John Gerrard Williams, arr.
(Piano)

Zanzig, Augustus D. (Arr.) — ECS 1906

"Once Long Ago"

SSA — Augustus D. Zanzig, arr.
(Piano)

Chapter V
Indices

The index lists in this chapter provide a series of cross references to the musical works listed and annotated in this study. The page number reference given after each title refers to a page in Chapter Four, where more complete information regarding that composition may be found.

A separate index for each of the following categories is provided: (1) titles of compositions alphabetically arranged, (2) number of vocal parts, (3) grade of difficulty (original works only), (4) compositions of extended length and (5) collections and their contents.

In the index of collections, works are cited under the heading of the collection title. Works so cited have not been annotated in Chapter Four, but they may be presumed to be of the same quality.

I. Index of Titles

Title	Composer	Page
April Is in My Mistress' Face	Morley-Davis	129
Arise, All Ye Servants of The Lord	Sweelinck-Macdonald	133
Ascendit Deus	Palestrina-Runkel	130
At Chrystemesse-tyde	Williams	127
At the Sweet Birth of Our Lord	Praetorius-Glaser	131
Ave Maria	Arcadelt-Davis	119
Ave Maria	Brahms	64
Ave Maria	Holst	83
Ave Maria	Hovhaness	85
Ave Maria	Kodaly	86
Ave Maria	Palestrina	98
Ave Maria	Vittoria-Taylor	134
Ave Regina	Menegali-Garabedian	128
Ave Verum	Des Préz	74
Ave Verum	Des Préz-Woodworth	124
Ave Verum	Faure	76
Away in a Manger	Terri (arr.)	133
Away! Thou Shalt Not Love Me	Wilbye	116
Babe is Born, A	Holst	83
Beautiful Saviour	Riegger (arr.)	132
Benedictus (fr. Mass O Admirabile Commercium)	Palestrina	99
Benedictus (fr. Missa Brevis)	Palestrina-Bement	130
Bird in Air Will Stray Afar	Brahms	68
Bird's Song, The	Frackenpohl (arr.)	125
Birth of Our Lord, The	Martinu	94
Blessed Are They that Dwell in Thy House	Brahms	64
Blessed Damozel, The	Debussy	73
Blessed is He Who Walks Not in the Paths of Godlessness	Schütz	107
Blow Winds, O Softly Blow	Mueller (arr.)	130
Bonnie Banks of Loch Lomond, The	West (arr.)	136
Bonnie George Campbell	Best (arr.)	119
Brother James' Air	Jacob (arr.)	126
Cantata from Proverbs	Milhaud	95
Cantate Domino	Hassler-Bement	126
Cantiones duarum Vocum	Lasso	89
Carol of the Bells	Leontovich-Wilhousky	128
Cease Your Bitter Weeping	Kodaly	87
Ce Moys de May	Jonequin-Finch	127
Ceremony of Carols, A	Britten	69
Chanson Joyeuse de Noel	Gevaert-Krone	125
Cherubic Song	Bortniansky-Ham	119
Child in the Manger	Treharne (sett.)	134
Children Come	Handl-Geer	126
Child's Book of Beasts, A	Berger	63

II. Index of Number of Parts

SA

Composer	Title	Page
Mendelssohn	I Would That My Love	94
Morley	See! Lovely Day Is Dawning	97
Peerson	Come Pretty Wag	101
Peerson	Cuckoo	101
Pergolesi	Stabat Mater	101
Praetorius (arr.)	In Dulci Jubilo	131
Purcell-Moffat	Sound the Trumpet (Welcome Song)	131
Rieger (arr.)	Beautiful Saviour (Crusader's Hymn)	132
Scarlatti	Stabat Mater	104
Schütz	Blessed Is He Who Walks Not in the Paths of Godlessness (Wohl dem, der nicht wandelt in rath der Gottlosen)	107
Schütz	Great is our Lord (Der Herr ist gross)	108
Schütz	O Gracious Lord Our God	108
Schütz-Hermann	Sing o Ye Saints (Ihr heiligen, lobsinget dem Herren)	108
Shaw	Sylvia Sleeps	109
Stanford	Vitue	111
Thiman (arr.)	O Brother Man (divisi)	133
Treharne (sett.)	Star Lullaby	134
Vaughn Williams	It Was a Lover and His Lass	113
West (arr.)	The Bonnie Banks of Loch Lomond	136
Williams (arr.)	Early One Morning	136

SSA

Composer	Title	Page
Abt	Night	61
Aichinger	Regina Coeli	61
Aichinger-Vene	Regina Coeli	119
Bach	Suscepit Israel (fr. Magnificat)	61
Barthelson (arr.)	Ding, Dong, Merrily on High	119
Bartok	Only Tell Me	63
Bell	The Flower of Jesse	63
Bennet (arr.)	All Creatures Now Are Merry Minded	119
Best (arr.)	Three Highland Airs	119
Bortniansky-Ham	Cherubic Song	119
Brahms	Come Away, Come Away, Death	65
Brahms-Trusler	Down Low in the Valley	120
	The Still of the Night	120
Brahms-Clough-Leighter	Four Love Songs	120
Brahms	Greetings (Der gartner-The Gardener)	66
Brahms	I Hear a Harp	66

Composer	Title	Page
Brahms	Ave Maria (Blessed Are They that Dwell in Thy House)	64
Brahms	Fidelin!	65
Brahms-Geer	Magdalena	120
Brahms	Mary's Pilgrimage	120
Brahms	O Bone Jesu	66
Brahms-Geer	Praise of Mary (Marias Lob)	120
Brahms	Queen of the Heavens (Regina Coeli)	67
Brahms	Roses are Blooming (Rosen in Blüthe)	67
Brahms-Geer	The Angelic Greeting (Der engelische gruss)	120
Brahms-Geer	The Hunter (Der jäger)	120
Brahms	The Nun (Die nonne)	68
Brahms-Geer	Three Chorales from Motets	121
Britten	Old Abram Brown	70
Byrd	Rejoice! Rejoice!	70
Byrd-Woodworth	Sacerdotes Domini	122
Chabrier	The Shulamite	71
Clarke (arr.)	I Saw Three Ships Come Sailing In	122
Copland-Fine	Ching-a-ring-chaw	123
Cui-Davis	Radiant Stars, Above the Mountains Flowing	123
Debussy	The Blessed Damozel	73
Debussy-Boyd	The Rain Falls on My Heart	124
Dello Joio	A Jubilant Song	73
Dickinson (arr.)	Angels o'er the Fields	124
Diemer	Fragments from the Mass	75
Dowland-Davis	Come Again, Sweet Love Doth Now Invite	124
Gasparini	Adoramus te	125
Geer (arr.)	Ding Dong! Merrily On High	125
Geer (arr.)	Noel, Nouvelet	125
Gevaert	Joyous Christmas Song	125
Gibbons	O Lord, Increase My Faith	125
Glaser (arr.)	The Twelve Days of Christmas	126
Haines	Dialogue from The Book of Job	79
Handel	Christus Factus Est	131
Handel	Pueri Concinite	126
Handel	Replenti Sunt Omnes	80
Harris	Whitman Triptych	81
Hasse	Miserere	81
Hassler	Cantate Domino	126
Holst	Ave Maria	83
Holst	Four Old English Carols	83
Holst	Funeral Chant	83
Holst	Hecuba's Lament	84
Holst	Hymn to Dionysus	84
Holst	Love On My Heart From Heaven Fell	85
Hovhaness	Ave Maria	85
Isaac	My Only Joy In All The World	126

III. Index of Grade of Difficulty

Easy

Composer	Title	Page
Holst	Four Old English Carols	83
Holst	Funeral Chant (Choral hymns from the *Rig Veda*) Group II	83
Holst	Love on My Heart from Heaven Fell	85
Hovhaness	Ave Maria	85
Ingegneri	Vere Languores Nostros (Surely He Hath Borne Our Grief)	86
Kodaly	Ave Maria	86
Kodaly	Cease Your Bitter Weeping	87
Lasso	Cantiones Duarum Vocum	89
Lawes	Come Lovely Chloris	90
Lawes	Gather Your Rosebuds	90
Lotti	Mass (in B^b)	92
Martini	A Measure to Pleasure Your Leisure	93
Martinu	The Birth of Our Lord	94
Mendelssohn	Ye Sons of Israel (Laudate Pueri)	95
Miller	Come Away, Sweet Love, and Play Thee	96
Miller	I Saw Lovely Phyllis	96
Miller	Welcome Sweet Pleasure	97
Monteverdi	Angelus ad pastores ait & Hodie Christus natus est (fr. *Sacre Cantiunculae*)	97
Morley	See! Lovely Day Is Dawning	97
Nelson	Jehovah, Hear Our Prayer (M-D)	98
Palestrina	Benedictus (M-D)	99
Palestrina	Crucifixus (fr. Mass *Assumpta est Maria*)	99
Palestrina	Magnificat (M-D)	100
Pergolesi	Stabat Mater	101
Pfautsch	Fanfare for Christmas	102
Pinkham	If Ye Love Me	103
Poulenc	Litanies	104
Scarlatti	Stabat Mater	104
Schubert	The Lord Is My Shepherd (Gott meine zunersicht)	105
Schuman	The Steadfast Heavens	106
Schütz	Blessed Is He Who Walks Not in the Paths of Godlessness (Wohl dem der nicht wandelt in rath der Gottlosen)	107
Schütz	Great Is Our Lord (Der Herr ist gross)	108
Schütz	O Gracious Lord Our God "Sing, O Ye Saints" (Ihr Heiligen Lobsinget dem Herren)	108
Shaw	With a Voice of Singing	109
Smith, M.	Lully, Lullay (M-D)	110
Thompson, R.	Come In (fr. *Frostiana*)	111
Thompson, R.	Pueri Hebraeorum	112

Composer	Title	Page
Vaughn Williams	Lullaby	113
Vaughn Williams	Magnificat	113
Verdi	Laudi alla Virgine Maria (Hymn to the Virgin)	114
Weelkes	Late in My Rash Accounting	115
Weelkes	The Gods Have Heard My Vows	115
Weelkes	Though My Carriage Be but Careless	116
Wilbye	Away! Thou Shalt Not Love Me	116
Wilbye	Come Shepherd Swains	116
Willan	Oh! Queen of Heaven (Regina Coeli, Letare)	117
Youll	Come, Merry Lads, Let Us Away	118
Youll	In the Merry Month of May	118

Difficult

Aichinger	Regina Coeli	61
Barber	The Virgin Martyrs	62
Brahms	Adoramus (We Adore Thee)	64
Brahms	Queen of the Heavens (Regina Coeli)	67
Brahms	Roses Are Blooming (Rosen in Blüthe)	67
Byrd	Rejoice! Rejoice!	70
Caplet	Messe a Trois Voix	71
Chabrier	The Shulamite	71
Couperin	Troisieme Lecon de Tenebres (Lamentations of Jeremiah)	72
Cui	Mystic Chorus (Chorus Mysticus)	72
Dello Joio	A Jubilant Song	73
Dello Joio	Song's End	74
Haines	Dialogue from the Book of Job	79
Harris	Whitman Triptych	81
Hasse	"Miserere"	81
Holst	Hecuba's Lament	84
Holst	Hymn to Dionysus	84
Kodaly	King Ladislaus' Men (Magyars and Germans)	87
Lasso	Adoramus Te Christe (We Adore Thee, O Lord)	88
Lasso	Three Psalms	90
Mechem	I Shall Not Care	94
Milhaud	Cantata from Proverbs	95
Palestrina	Ave Maria	98
Palestrina	Innocentes pro Christo	100
Peters	Quatuor Motetta	102
Pinkham	Three Lenten Poems of Richard Crashaw	103
Schubert	Serenade	105
Schuman, W.	Prelude for Women's Voices	106

IV. Index of Works of Extended Length

V. Index of Recommended Collections

A Cappella Singer, The. A Collection of Motets, Madrigals, Chansons, Carols, Ayres, Ballets, etc. Edited by H. Clough-Leighter. Boston: E. C. Schirmer Music Company, 1936.

Composer	Title
Bortniansky	Lo, a Voice to Heaven Sounding
Brahms	Charm Me Asleep
Cui	Radiant Stars, about the Mountains

Composer	Title
Davis, K. K.	Come, Lasses and Lads
Davis, K. K.	The Beetle's Wedding
Davis, K. K.	The Old Woman and the Pedlar
Davis, K. K.	Tiritomba
Davis, K. K.	'Tween the Mount and Deep, Deep Vale
Davis, K. K.	Touro-louro-louro!
Dowland	Come Again! Sweet Love Doth Now Invite
Geer	Christ the Lord Hath Risen
Geer	In Dulci Jubilo
Gevaert	O Filii et Filiae
Gevaert	The Slumber of the Infant Jesus
Gibbons	The Silver Swan
Knab	Oh, Show Me How the Gentlemen Ride
Lasso	Adoramus Te, Christe
Lotti	Vere Languores Nostros
Makarov	An Angel Said to Mary
Morley	Now Is the Month of Maying
Morley	Sing We and Chant It
Palestrina	Jesu! Rex Admirabilis
Praetorius	Rejoice, ye Christian Men, Rejoice
Purcell	With Drooping Wings, ye Cupids Come
Vittoria	Tanquam Agnus
Weelkes	On the Plains, Fairy Trains
Weelkes	Strike It Up, Tabor
Weelkes	The Nightingale
Wilbye	Adieu, Sweet Amarillis
Wilbye	Weep, O Mine Eyes

Art of Polyphonic Song, The. Compositions of the Sixteenth and Seventeenth Centuries for Two to Eight Parts. Edited by Hans David. New York: G. Schirmer, 1940.

Composer	Title
Byrd	In Crystal Towers
Ferrabosco	In Thee O Lord
Handl	Trahe Me Post Te
Handl	Virgines Prudentes
Hassler	Core Mio
Hofhaimer	Tu ne Quaesieris
Hofhaimer	Vitam quae Faciant Beatiorem
Lasso	Beatus Homo
Lasso	Exspectatio Justorum
Lasso	Qui Sequitur Me
Lasso	Tragico Tecti Syrmate
Lecouteux	Louange et Glorie
Le Jeune	Le Courant des Faux
Le Jeune	O Seigneur, J'espars
Le Jeune	Quant la Terre au Printemps
Morley	Go, Ye, My Canzonets
Morley	O Sleep, Fond Fancy
Palestrina	Alma Redemptoris
Palestrina	Esercizio Sopra la Scala
Praetorius	Puer Natus in Bethlehem
Senfl	Ego ipse Consolabor Vos
Sweelinck	Io mi Son Giovinetta
Sweelinck	Voici du Gai Printemps

Composer	Title
Weelkes	Come Sirrah Jack, ho
Weelkes	Ha ha, This World Doth Pass
Weelkes	Lo, Country Sports
Weelkes	The Nightingale, the Organ of Delight
Wilbye	As Fair as Morn

Carols for the Seasons. Settings by Healey Willan. St. Louis: Concordia Publishing House, 1959.

All My Heart Today Rejoices
Ascended Is Our God and Lord
Away in a Manger
Beautiful Savior
Child in the Manger
Come, Souls, Behold Today
From Heaven High I Come to Earth
Good Christian Men, Rejoice
He Whom Joyous Shepherds Praised
Lord's My Shepherd, The (Brother James' air)
Love Came Down at Christmas
Maria Walks amid the Thorn
Now Let the Heavens Be Joyful
Oh, Come, All Ye Faithful
Oh, How Beautiful the Sky
O Little Town of Bethlehem
Prepare the Way, O Zion
Shepherds Watched Their Flocks by Night
Sing to the Lord of Harvest
Spring Carol, A
This Joyful Eastertide
What Star is This, with Beams so Bright

Canzonets for Two Voices by Thomas Morley. Edited by Edmund H. Fellowes. London: Stainer and Bell.

Fire and Lightning from Heaven
Flora, Wilt Thou Torment Me?
Go Ye, My Cansonets
I Go Before, My Darling
In Nets of Golden Wires
I Should for Grief and Anguish
Leave Now, Mine Eyes
Lo, Here Another Love
Miraculous Love's Wounding
O Thou that Art So Cruel
Sweet Nymph, Come to Thy Lover
When Lo, by Break of Morning

Canzonettens. Eleven Canzonetts for Three Equal Voices by Claudio Monteverdi. Edited by Hilman Trede. Kassel: Bärenreiter.

Chi Vuol Veder un Bosco
Come Faro Cour Mio quando mi Parto
Corse a la Morte il
Gia Mi Credevim

Giu Lia quel Petto Giace
Godi pur del Bel Sen
Hor Care Canzonette
Io mi Vivea
Io Son Fenice
Si Come Crescon
Vita de l'Alura Mia

Eighteen Duets for Soprano and Alto from the Cantatas by Johann S. Bach. English translated and edited by Henry S. Drinker. Philadelphia: University of Pennsylvania Choral Series.

Ach Herr, mein Gott, vergib mir's doch
Beruft Gott selbst, so muss der segen
Den tod niemand zwingen kunnt
Die armut, so Gott auf sich nimmt
Domine Deus, agnus Dei, (Latin only)
Entziehe dich eilends, mein herze, der welt
Er kennt die rechten freudenstunden
Gedenk an Jesu bittern tod
Herr, du siehst statt guter warke
Herr Gott Vaterm mein starker held
Herz, zerreiss des mammons kette
Ich folge dir nach
Ihr klaget mif seufzen, ich jauchze mit schall
Nimm mich mir und gib mich dir
Nun komm, der Heiden Heiland
Weichet, weichet, furcht und schrecken
Wenn des kreuzes bitterkeiten
Wir eilen mit schwachen, doch emsigen schritten

Laudate Pueri. Sacred Music of the Sixteenth Century. Edited by Donald Tovey. London: Augener, 1910.

Composer	Title
Agostini	Adoramus Te
Constantini	Confitemini Domino
Croce	Et Resurrexit
Gabrieli	Crucifixus
Lasso	Adoramus Te
Lasso	Agimus Tibi Gratias
Lasso	Alleluja Laus et Gloria
Lasso	Benedictus Qui Venit
Lasso	Expandi Manus
Lasso	Hodie Apparuit in Israel
Lasso	Ipsa te Cogat Pietas
Lasso	In Pace in Idipsum Dormiam
Lasso	Oculus non Vidit
Lasso	Sancti Mei
Mozart	Alleluja
Mozart	Ave Maria
Mozart	Kyrie Eleison
Palestrina	Adoramus Te
Palestrina	Benedictus Qui Venit

Composer	Title
Palestrina	Benedictus Qui Venit
Palestrina	Confitemini Domino
Palestrina	Crucifixus
Palestrina	Hodie Christus Natus Est
Palestrina	Jesu Rex Admirabilis
Palestrina	Pleni sunt Coeli
Palestrina	Salve Regina
Palestrina	Tua Jesu Dilectio
Vittoria (Victoria, T. L.)	Accende Lumen Sensibus
Vittoria	Christe Eleison
Vittoria	Duo Seraphim
Vittoria	O Sacrum Convivium
Vittoria	O Vos Omnes

Madrigals for Treble Voices. Edited and arranged by Donald Malin. New York: The B. F. Wood Music Company, Inc., 1964.

de Wert	The Messenger of Love
Dowland	A Shepherd in a Shade
Gastoldi	Maidens Fair of Mantua's City
Gibbons	The Silver Swan
Lasso	My Heart to Thee Now Makes Its Plea
Morley	It Was a Lover and His Lass
Morley	Now Is the Month of Maying
Vecchi	Let All Who Sing Be Merry
Weelkes	Since Robin Hood
Weelkes	Some Men Desire Spouses
Weelkes	To Shorten Winter's Sadness

Mediaeval and Renaissance Choral Music for Equal Voices A Cappella. Edited by Georgia Stevens. Boston: Mc Laughlin and Reilly Company, 1940.

Animuccia	Kyrie
Anonymous	Alleluia-Angelus Domini
Anonymous	Alleluia Psallet
Anonymous	Hymn of St. Adalbert
Anonymous	Catalan Folk Songs
Anonymous	German Flagellants' Hymn
Anonymous	O Miranda Dei Garitas
Anonymous	Puellare Gremium
Anonymous	Sanctus
Dufay	Flos Florum
Dunstable	Quam Pulchra Es
Lasso	Benedictus
Leoninus	Haec Dies
Obrecht	Missa Sine Nomine
Obrecht	Qui cum Patre
Ott	Dies Est Laetitiae
Ott	On This Our Joyful Holiday
Palestrina	Pueri Hebraeorum
Tallis	Sancte Deus
Taverner	Audivi

Composer	Title
Taverner	Gloria in Excelsis
Vittoria	Judas Mercator
Vittoria	Una Hora

Morning Star Choir Book, The. A Collection of Unison and Two-part Music for Treble or Male Voices. Compiled and edited by Paul Thomas. St. Louis: Concordia, 1957.

Bach	Beside Thy Manger Here I Stand
Bach	Jesus, Refuge of the Weary
Bach	Let All the Multitudes of Light
Bach	The Only Son from Heaven
Bender	Built on the Rock the Church Doth Stand
Bender	Come, Ye Faithful, Raise the Strain
Bender	O Christ, Thou Lamb of God
Brahms	O Jesus, Joy of Loving Hearts
Bouman	Behold, the Lamb of God
Buxtehude	Arise, Sons of the Kingdom
Buxtehude	To God the Anthem Raising
Franck	Ascended Is Our God and Lord
Greene	Thou Visitest the Earth
Gumpeltzhaimer	Go Ye into All the World
Handel	Daughter of Zion
Lenel	All Praise to God Who Reigns Above
Lenel	Loving Shepherd of the Sheep
Marcello	Oh, Hold Thou Me Up
Mozart	Alleluia
Pachelbel	What God Ordains Is Always Good
Schop	How Lovely Shines the Morning Star
Tunder	Wake, Awake, for Night Is Flying
Vaugh Williams	Unto Him That Loved Us
Vierdanck	Glory to God in the Highest
Willan	Glory Be to God on High
Willan	Holy, Holy, Holy
Wolff	Come, Holy Spirit, Come
Wolff	Sing with Joy, Glad Voices Lift

Renaissance to Baroque. Three Centuries of Choral Music. Selected and edited by Lehman Engel. New York: Harold Flammer, Inc., 1962.

Brihuega	Domingo, Fuese Tu Amiga (Domingo, Your Friend Is Gone)
Brudieu	O Jos Claros y Suenos (Eyes So Clear, So Calm, So Tender)
Certon	Benedictus from Mass: Regnum Mundi
Des Prêz	Ave Verum Corpus
Dowland	Weep No More, Sad Fountains
Dunstable	Quam Pulchra Es
Farmer	Fair Phyllis I Saw
Lasso	Un Jour Ves un Foulon (Once I Saw a Fuller)
Monteverdi	Filli Care a Amata

Composer	Title
	(Filli, Fairest and Most Dear)
Nanino	Laetamini in Domino
Palestrina	Congratulamini Nihi
Scheidt	Gib uns heut unser taglich brodt (Give Us This Day Our Daily Bread)
Urrede	De Vos i de mi Quexoso
Whythorne	I Have Ere This Time

Chapter VI

Summary, Conclusions and Recommendations for Further Study

In this study, certain historical factors and critical considerations of music for women's voices were investigated and interpreted. These considerations, in turn, prompted speculation about the need for other investigations of a related nature which might be of value.

I. Summary

Statement of the problem. The purposes of this study were (1) to give a brief account of the history of choral singing by women; (2) to establish and validate a set of criteria for selecting outstanding choral works which were originally composed for female or high voices; (3) to annotate each work selected according to the general content of its musical elements and style; (4) to provide catalog-type information which included number of parts, range, publisher, grade of difficulty and type of accompaniment; and (5) to establish and implement a system of multiple cross indexes of those scores examined.

Importance of the study. The growth in the number of women's choral organizations within the last several decades has been significant. The musical leadership of such groups necessarily has involved a great number of men and women who have heretofore had only limited knowledge of the literature for such a vocal combination. Along with this rapid increase in such choral groups, there has been a parallel increase in the number of compositions written for treble choirs by contemporary composers, as well as in the publication of previously inaccessible works by earlier composers. All of these factors underscored the urgent need for a comprehensive bibliography prepared with some degree of discriminating selectivity.

Method of research. Numerous sources were consulted in an effort to ascertain the varying role permitted women in the history of choral performance. This historical investigation provided significant information in at least two ways. First, it disproved a common belief that choral groups comprised solely of women were rare prior to the nineteenth century and that original music of earlier styles and composition techniques for this vocal combination was practically nonexistent. The authentication of choral performance by women prior to the nineteenth century provided a logical basis to investigate what music was available to them. Second, it resulted in the discovery of a substantial body of worthy literature that had been largely ignored.

After determining that a significant body of literature was available for female choral organizations, a recommended list of available compositions was compiled and annotated. These compositions were deemed to be of the highest musical quality. To validate and substantiate the works listed, it was necessary to evolve defensible criteria. The method of research applied to this portion of the study was an investigation into the nature of esthetics. Pertinent literature dealing with philosophy, esthetics and music criticism was examined in constructing the criteria employed.

To make this list of maximum value to the conductor searching for appropriate literature, detailed annotations of the works listed under the category of music originally composed for women's voices were included. Extensive investigation of related topics revealed that there exists no other such annotated bibliography for music for women's voices. Each work listed was carefully examined and analyzed. In addition, a substantial number of these works were heard or conducted in actual performance by various women's choral organizations at the collegiate level. An approximately equal number of works "arranged" or "edited" for performance by female voices was also listed, but not annotated in this study. All of these non-original works underwent the same critical analysis as the "original" works and were found to meet the same quality standard. Finally, a series of indices which provide cross references and category listings and an index of recommended collections and their contents were provided.

II. Conclusions

Although the literature available to the mixed choir is more extensive, the choral literature for all-female choral groups is neither meager nor inferior. The historical record of female choral performance reveals that not only has there always been substantial participation in this activity, but that important composers such as Palestrina, Lasso, Pergolesi and Brahms have contributed to the repertoire and were impressed by the quality of such singing in their respective times. Since the nineteenth century, spurred chiefly by the public schools and institutions of higher learning which have fostered choral singing, the number of women's choirs has increased significantly in quantity and quality. This has been reflected in a parallel increase in the number of compositions written for such organizations, many by highly recognized composers.

In attempting to determine a valid set of criteria for a selected list such as that included in this study, the matter of subjective versus objective factors in analysis, response and evaluation was of critical importance. After examining many writings on the subject of esthetics, it was concluded that it is virtually impossible to find agreement in these areas.

Several philosophical and esthetic theories were then examined as an alternate method of developing criteria for selection. It was determined that the most desirable theory for establishing criteria was that of isolationism, which is based on objective analysis and stresses that the most reliable standard of judgment is that determined by the expert in the field. According to this theory, the significance of music is tonal, not extra-musical; the structure of music is the most important criterion for establishing a standard of "good". For these reasons, the theory of isolationism was considered to be the most defensible basis for making the type of value judgments employed in this study.

III. Recommendations for Further Study

The suggestions below indicate some related areas where research or further investigation would be profitable:

1. Similar annotated bibliographies of choral music for male voices.
2. Similar annotated bibliographies of choral music for mixed voices.
3. An annotated bibliography of recommended vocal selections for children.

4. Similar annotated bibliographies of recorded compositions for use in music appreciation or music literature courses at high school and collegiate levels.

5. Studies to determine how choral program building can be made more effective, both for performers and audiences.

6. Studies to categorize the specific compositions that can be used to develop various vocal skills and musical concepts for choral singers.

7. Studies to determine more articulate standards by which music may be judged.

8. Addition of selected bibliographies to the state music manuals which provide the choice of literature for various state festivals and programs.

Bibliography

Books

Apel, Willi. Harvard Dictionary of Music. Cambridge, Harvard University Press, 1960.

Bacon, Ernst. Words on Music. Syracuse, Syracuse University Press, 1960.

Barzun, Jacques. The Pleasures of Music. N. Y., Viking Press, 1960.

Biehl, Herbert. Die Stimmkunst. Leipzig, Kistner and Siegel, 1931.

Birkhoff, George D. Aesthetic Measure. Cambridge, Harvard University Press, 1933.

Buck, Percy C. The Scope of Music. London, Oxford University Press, 1927.

Bukofzer, Manfred. Music in the Baroque Era. N. Y., W. W. Norton, 1947.

Cain, Noble. Choral Music and Its Practice. N. Y., M. Witmark and Sons, 1932.

Chambers, E. K. The Mediaeval Stage. Oxford, Clarendon Press, 1903.

Chaves, Carlos. Musical Thought. Cambridge, Harvard University Press, 1961.

David, Hans (ed.). The Art of Polyphonic Song. N. Y., G. Schirmer, 1940.

Davison, A. T. The Technique of Choral Composition. Cambridge, Harvard University Press, 1945.

Dewey, John. Art as Experience. N. Y., Minton, Balch, 1934.

Dorian, Frederick L. The History of Music in Performance. N. Y., W. W. Norton, 1942.

Drinker, Sophie. Music and Women. N. Y., Coward-McCann, 1948.

Elson, Arthur. Women's Work in Music. Boston, L. C. Page, 1903.

Fellowes, Edmund H. The English Madrigal Composers. London, Oxford University Press, 1921.

Ferguson, Donald. Music as Metaphor. Minneapolis, University of Minnesota Press, 1960.

Fuller-Maitland, J. A. The Consort of Music: A Study of Interpretation and Ensemble. Oxford, Clarendon Press, 1915.

Grout, Donald J. A Short History of Opera. N. Y., Columbia University Press, 1947.

Hanslick, Edward. The Beautiful in Music. Trans. Gustave Cohen. London, Novello, 1885.

Harman, Alec, and Anthony Milner. Man and His Music. 3 vols. Fairlawn, N. J., Essential Books, 1959.

Heyl, Bernard C. New Bearings in Esthetics and Art Criticism. New Haven, Yale University Press, 1943.

Hilpisch, Stephanus. History of Benedictine Nuns. Collegeville, Minn., St. John's Abbey Press, 1958.

Hirt, Charles C. Criteria for the Composing, Arranging and Editing of Choral Literature for the Senior High School Mixed Chorus. Los Angeles, Affiliated Musicians, 1954.

Holst, Imogene. Gustave Holst. London, Oxford University Press, 1938.

Hooker, Edward W. Music as a Part of Female Education. Boston, Marvin Press, 1843.

Jeppesen, Knud. Counterpoint: The Polyphonic Style of the Sixteenth Century. Trans. Glen Haydon. Englewood Cliffs, N. J., Prentice-Hall, 1930.

Julian, Jean. Dictionary of Hymnology. London, John Murray, 1925.

Knapp, J. Merill (ed.). Selected List of Music for Men's Voices. Princeton, Princeton University Press, 1952.

Lang, Paul H. Music in Western Civilization. N. Y., W. W. Norton, 1941.

Langer, Susanne K. Feeling and Form. N. Y., Charles Scribner's Sons, 1953.

Langer, Susanne K. Philosophy in a New Key. Cambridge, Harvard University Press, 1951.

Leichtentritt, Hugo. Music, History and Ideas. Cambridge, Harvard University Press, 1954.

Locke, Arthur W., and Charles K. Fassett (eds.). Selected List of Choruses for Women's Voices. Northampton, Mass., Smith College, 1964.

Manning, Rosemary. From Holst to Britten. London, Worker's Music, 1949.

Meese, Arthur. Choirs and Choral Music. N. Y., Charles Scribner's Sons, 1911.

Mendl, R. W. S. The Soul of Music. London, Rockliff Publishing, 1950.

Meyer, Leonard B. Emotion and Meaning in Music. Chicago, University of Chicago Press, 1956.

Moore, Douglas. From Madrigal to Modern Music. N. Y., W. W. Norton, 1942.

Mueller, John. The American Symphony Orchestra. Bloomington, University of Indiana Press, 1951.

Parker, Dewitt. The Principles of Aesthetics. N. Y., Silver Burdett, 1920.

Rader, Melvin (ed.). A Modern Book of Aesthetics. N. Y., Henry Holt, 1952.

Reese, Gustave. Music in the Middle Ages. N. Y., W. W. Norton, 1954.

Reese, Gustave. Music in the Renaissance. N. Y., W. W. Norton, 1954.

Ritter, Fanny R. Woman as a Musician. N. Y., Edward Schuberth, 1876.

Sachs, Curt. The Wellsprings of Music. The Hague, Netherlands, Martinus Nijhoff, 1962.

Schoen, Max. Art and Beauty. N. Y., MacMillan, 1932.

Scott, Charles Kennedy. Madrigal Singing. London, Oxford University Press, 1931.

Sessions, Roger. The Musical Experience of Composer, Performer, Listener. Princeton, Princeton University Press, 1950.

Strunck, Oliver (ed.). Source Readings in Music History. N. Y., W. W. Norton, 1950.

Thompson, Oscar. Practical Musical Criticism. N. Y., M. Witmark and Sons, 1934.

Thomson, Virgil, The Art of Judging Music. N. Y., Alfred A. Knopf, 1948.

Tovey, Donald F. Vocal Music. Vol. V of Essays in Musical Analysis. 5 vols. London, Oxford University Press, 1937.

Tovey, Donald F. The Main Streams of Art and Other Essays. N. Y., Oxford University Press, 1949.

Trever, Albert A. History of Ancient Civilization. 2 vols. N. Y., Harcourt, Brace, 1939.

Weinstock, Herbert. Music as an Art. N. Y., Harcourt, Brace, 1953.

Young, Karl. The Drama of the Medieval Church. 2 vols. N. Y., Oxford University Press, 1933.

Young, Percy M. The Choral Tradition. London, Hutchinson, 1962.

Publications of Learned Societies and Other Organizations

Broudy, Harry S. "A Realistic Philosophy of Music Education," Basic Concepts in Music Education. Chicago, University of Chicago Press, 1958. Fifty-seventh Yearbook of the National Society for the Study of Education, Part I:62-87.

Christy, Van A. "Evaluation of Choral Music," Contributions to Education, New York, Bureau of Publications, Teachers College, Columbia University, 1948. No. 885.

Mueller, John H. "Music and Education: A Sociological Approach," Basic Concepts in Music Education. Chicago, University of Chicago Press, 1958. Fifty-seventh Yearbook of the National Society for the Study of Education. Part I:88-122.

Tolhurst, J. B. L. (ed.). The Ordinale and Customary of the Benedictine Nuns of Barking Abbey. London, Henry Bradshaw Society, 1927. LXV. (2 vols.)

Periodicals

Bernstein, Leonard. "Speaking of Music," The Atlantic Monthly. Dec. 1957. 104-106.

Bullough, Edward. "Psychical Distance as a Factor in Art and as an Aesthetic Principle," British Journal of Psychology. V:II, pp. 87-118. 1912.

Dewey, John. "Meaning of Value," Journal of Philosophy. Feb. 1925.

Reimer, Bennett. "Leonard Meyer's Theory of Value and Greatness in Music," Journal of Research in Music Education. Fall, 1962. X:2, pp. 87-99.

Schoen, Max. "Psychological Problems in Musical Art," Journal of Research in Music Education. III (1):27-39. Spring, 1955.

Vernon, P. E. "A Method for Measuring Musical Taste," Journal of Applied Psychology. XIV (4):355-362. April, 1930.

Essays and Articles in Collections

Angles, Higini. "Gregorian Chant," New Oxford History of Music. Dom Anselem Hughes, ed. Vol. II, Early Medieval Music up to 1300. New York, Oxford University Press, 1954. pp. 92-127.

Auden, W. H. "Notes on Music and Opera," The Dyer's Hand and Other Essays. N. Y., Random House, 1962. pp. 465-474.

Butler, Samuel. "Note Books," An Anthology of Music Criticism. Compiled by Norman Demuth. London, Eyre and Spottiswoode, 1947. pp 99-100.

Handschin, Jacques. "Trope, Sequence and Conductus," New Oxford History of Music. Dom Anselem Hughes, ed. Vol. II, Early Medieval Music up to 1300. N. Y., Oxford University Press, 1954. pp. 128-174.

Harrison, Frank. "English Polyphony," New Oxford History of Music. Dom Anselm Hughes, ed. Vol. III, Ars Nova and the Renaissance 1300-1540. N. Y., Oxford University Press, 1954. pp. 303-348.

Kinkeldey, Otto. "Equal Voices in the a capella Period," Essays on Music. Cambridge, Harvard College, 1957.

Parry, (Sir) Hubert. "The Significance of Monteverdi," An Anthology of Music Criticism, compiled by Norman Demuth. London, Eyre and Spottiswoode, 1947. pp. 17-22.

Smoldon, W. L. "Liturgical Drama," New Oxford History of Music.

Dom Anselm Hughes, ed. Vol. II, Early Medieval Music up to 1300. N. Y., Oxford University Press, 1954. pp. 175-219.

Unpublished Materials

Coffin, Roscoe. "A Handbook of Materials for Choral Programs," Unpublished Ed. D. dissertation, Columbia University, N. Y., 1950.

Bowman, Horace B. "The Castrati Singers and Their Music," Unpublished Ph. D. dissertation. Bloomington, The University of Indiana, 1951.

Johnson, Gerald W. "A Study of Choral Practices and Procedures in Methodist Senior Colleges," Unpublished Mus. A. D. dissertation, Boston University, 1958.

Kingston, Robert J. "A Study of Choral Music Styles Including Current Listing of Available Octavo Music," Unpublished master's thesis, Boston University, 1954.

Schwadron, Abraham. "An Interpretation of Philosophy and Aesthetics for Contemporary Music Education," Unpublished Mus. A. D. dissertation, Boston University, 1962.

Appendix

Key to Abbreviations Used in Chapter IV

A	alto
adapt.	adapted
AJ	Arthur Jordan Choral Series
AMP	Associated Music Publishers, Inc.
APS	A. P. Schmidt
arr	arranger
AST	Arthur S. Talmadge
ATD	Archibald T. Davison
Au	Augener, Ltd.
Bank	Annie Bank
BC	basso continuo
Bir	C. C. Birchard Company
BM	Boston Music Company
BoHa	Boosey and Hawkes
Bourne	Bourne, Inc.
Brodt	Brodt Music Company
CF	Carl Fischer
Ch	J. & W. Chester
Coll	collection
Colombo	Franco Colombo
Con	Concordia Publishing House
Cur	Curwen and Sons
DeRing	DeRing Antwerp
Diff.	difficult
Durand	Durand et Cie
ECS	E. C. Schirmer Music Company
ed.	edited
EHF	Edmund Horace Fellowes
EHG	E. Harold Geer
ELKAN	Elkan-Vogel Company
ESR	E. C. Schirmer, Radcliffe Choral Series
ESV	E. C. Schirmer, Vassar Choral Series
Flammer	Harold Flammer
Galaxy	Galaxy Music Corporation
GB	Gwynn Bement
Gray	H. W. Gray
GS	G. Schirmer Music Company
GWW	G. Wallace Woodworth
HC-L	H. Clough-Leighter
JF	J. Fischer and Brothers
Kalmus	Edwin F. Kalmus
KKD	Katherine K. Davis
LG	Lawson-Gould
Marks	Edward B. Marks Music Corporation
MCD	Music Press, Dessoff Choir Series

Med.	Medium
Mercury	Mercury Music Corporation
Mills	Mills Music, Inc.
MP	Music Press
MR	McLaughlin and Reilly
MS	mezzo-soprano
N	Novello and Company, Ltd.
Ol-Dit	Oliver-Ditson
Orch.	orchestra
Ox	Oxford University Press
P	C. F. Peters
Presser	Theodore Presser Company
Pro-Art	Pro-Art
Remick	Remick Music Company
Rev.	revised
Ric	G. Ricordi
Row	R. D. Row Music Company
S	soprano
SB	Stainer and Bell
Schmidt	Schmidt-Hall and McCreary
Southern	Southern Music Publishers Company, Inc.
Summy	Summy-Birchard Publishing Company
transcr.	transcriber
UPC	University of Pennsylvania Choral Series
Unacc.	unaccompanied
VG	Victoria Glaser
W	M. Witmark and Sons
WGW	W. Gillies Whittaker
WLSM	World Library of Sacred Music
Wood	B. F. Wood

The following diagram illustrates the octave position system employed to designate pitch ranges.

Addresses of Publishers

Arthur Jordan Choral Series, obtain through Marks.

Associated Music Publishers, Inc., 1 West 47th Street, New York 36, N. Y.

A. P. Schmidt, obtain through Schmidt, Hall & McCreary.

Augener, Ltd., London, obtain through Galaxy.

Annie Bank, Amsterdam, obtain through World Library of Sacred Music.

C. C. Bichard Company, obtain through Summy-Birchard Company.

Boston Music Company, 116 Bolyston Street, Boston, Mass.

Boosey and Hawkes, Oceanside, N. Y.

Bourne, Inc., 136 West 52nd Street, New York 19, N. Y.

Brodt Music Company, Charlotte, N. C.

Broude Brothers, 56 West 45th Street, New York 36, N. Y.

J. and W. Chester, London, obtain through Marks.

Franco Colombo, 16 West 61st Street, New York 23, N. Y.

Concordia Publishing House, 3558 South Jefferson Avenue, St. Louis 18, Mo.

Curwen and Sons, London, obtain through G. Schirmer.

DeRing Antwerp, obtain through Eklan-Vogel.

Durand et Cie, Paris, obtain through Elkan-Vogel.

Elkan-Vogel Company, 1716 Sansome Street, Philadelphia 3, Penn.

Carl Fischer, 62 Cooper Square, New York 3, N. Y.

J. Fischer and Brothers, Harristown Road, Glen Rock, N. J.

Harold Flammer, 251 West 19th Street, New York, N. Y.

Galaxy Music Corporation, 2121 Broadway, New York 23, N. Y.

H. W. Gray, 159 East 48th Street, New York 17, N. Y.

Lawson-Gould, obtain through G. Schirmer.

Edwin F. Kalmus, 421 West 28th Street, New York 1, N. Y.

Edward B. Marks Music Corporation, 136 West 52nd Street, New York 19, N. Y.

Music Press, obtain through Presser.

Mercury Music Corporation, obtain through Presser.

Mills Music, Inc., 1619 Broadway, New York, N. Y.

McLaughlin and Reilly Company, 252 Huntington Avenue, Boston, Mass.

Novello and Company, Ltd., London, obtain through Gray.

Oliver Ditson, obtain through Presser.

Oxford University Press, 147 Fifth Avenue, New York 16, N. Y.

C. F. Peters Corporation, 373 Park Avenue South, New York 16, N. Y.

Theodore Presser Company, Presser Place, Bryn Mawr, Penn.

Pro-Art Publication, 469 Union Avenue, Westbury, Long Island, N. Y.

Remick Music Company, obtain through M. Whitmark.

G. Ricordi, obtain through Colombo.

R. D. Row Music Company, obtain through Boston Music Company.

E. C. Schirmer, 600 Washington Street, Boston, Mass.

G. Schirmer Music Company, 4 East 49th Street, New York 17, N. Y.

Schmidt, Hall & McCreary, 527 Park Avenue, Minneapolis 15, Minn.

Southern Music Publishers Company, Inc., 1619 Boradway, New York 19, N. Y.

Stainer and Bell, obtain through Galaxy.

Summy-Birchard Publishing Company, 1834 Ridge Avenue, Evanston, Ill.

University of Pennsylvania Choral Series, Free Library of Pennsylvania, Logan Square, Philadelphia 3, Penn.

M. Witmark and Sons, 488 Madison Avenue, New York, N. Y.

B. F. Wood, obtain through Mills.

World Library of Sacred Music, 1846 Westwood Avenue, Cincinnati 14, Ohio.

Index